Beating the Odds

Beating the Odds:

Keys to Overcoming the Hidden Barriers to College Success

CHERYL KROLL

BALBOA.
PRESS
A DIVISION OF HAY HOUSE

Balboa Press books may be ordered through booksellers or by contacting:

Balboa Press
A Division of Hay House
1663 Liberty Drive
Bloomington, IN 47403
www.balboapress.com
1-(877) 407-4847

Because of the dynamic nature of the Internet, any web addresses or links contained in this book may have changed since publication and may no longer be valid. The views expressed in this work are solely those of the author and do not necessarily reflect the views of the publisher, and the publisher hereby disclaims any responsibility for them.

The author of this book does not dispense medical advice or prescribe the use of any technique as a form of treatment for physical, emotional, or medical problems without the advice of a physician, either directly or indirectly. The intent of the author is only to offer information of a general nature to help you in your quest for emotional and spiritual well-being. In the event you use any of the information in this book for yourself, which is your constitutional right, the author and the publisher assume no responsibility for your actions.

Certain stock imagery © Thinkstock.
Any people depicted in stock imagery provided by Thinkstock are models, and such images are being used for illustrative purposes only.

Printed in the United States of America

ISBN: 978-1-4525-6862-1 (e)
ISBN: 978-1-4525-6861-4 (sc)
ISBN: 978-1-4525-6863-8 (hc)

Library of Congress Control Number: 2013902686

Balboa Press rev. date: 3/11/2013

He has achieved success who has lived well, laughed often and loved much;
who has gained the respect of intelligent men and the love of little children;
who has filled his niche and accomplished his task;
who has left the world better than he found it, whether by
an improved poppy, a perfect poem, or a rescued soul;
who has never lacked appreciation of earth's beauty or failed to express it;
who has always looked for the best in others and given the best he had;
whose life was an inspiration; whose memory a benediction.

--Bessie A. Stanley
December 11, 1905

TABLE OF CONTENTS

INTRODUCTION

Why Read This Book?

The answer to this question is very simple: because it will help you. As college students, you will have the opportunity to take a variety of courses, seminars, or workshops that will expose you to those factors we typically associate with college success, namely, metacognitive strategies (i.e., learning how to learn), goal setting, time management, memory and concentration, study skills, health and wellness, and personal relationships – to name but a few. If my experience as a community college professor and counselor has taught me anything at all, however, it is that the aforementioned topics tell only half the story when it comes to success in college. The other half is much more subjective but has come to light in just about every conversation I have had with a student whose grade point average is not where it needs to be. More often than not, I learn that one or more of the personal barriers discussed in this book is also significantly affecting my students' academic performance.

To address this issue, I began writing a series of short articles on these topics, but when I noticed how quickly they were disappearing from the literature bins into which I had placed them outside my office, I decided to write a short book about them, not just because so many students were obviously dealing with these hidden barriers to success but because many more would, in all probability, face at least one of them in the future. To this end, my overarching aim in providing you with the material contained on the following pages is to help each of you understand the personal barriers you may be facing and to provide you with some concrete strategies for addressing them. All it takes to do so are the resources you already have at your disposal as college students: the time to do the work, the willingness to make the effort, and the determination to succeed.

If you invest the time and effort needed to understand and ultimately conquer these personal barriers, you will be well on your way to realizing the dreams that your college education is uniquely designed to help you achieve. In the end, I can't think of a better reason to read this book. If you agree with me, by all means, take the first step and read on ... .

1

When You Just Can't Beat the Blues:

Understanding Depression

"That was the most depressing movie I ever saw!"
"I just got my grade in Professor Johnson's class, and I'm so depressed!"
"Spending time with my mom always depresses me."

Depression: it's a word we often hear bandied about in casual conversations, and, in all likelihood, it's a word each of us frequently uses to describe our reactions to specific events and/or people. On a much more serious note, however, it's also a word that describes a very treatable medical condition that affects millions of people, male and female, around the world, many of whom don't even know they have it and many of whom are not achieving their goals because of it. According to the National Institute of Mental Health (2011), a significant number of these same individuals first experience depression in college, though, for a variety of reasons, they very rarely seek treatment during this time. If you are experiencing the symptoms of depression, you may believe it is normal for you to feel this way, you may think there is nothing you can do about it, or you may fear that you will be judged unfavorably because of it (NIMH, 2011). Thus, I want to begin this chapter by reassuring you that, like any other medical condition, depression is, in fact, highly treatable and is in no way a reflection of an individual's character, ability or worth. This point will become readily evident as we examine depression in much greater detail in the discussion that follows.

Defining the Problem: What is Depression?

Insofar as it is possible, I am going to try to avoid employing any clinical definitions in this book because they can be misleading and/ or stigmatizing. Instead, I will define each chapter's personal barrier in layperson's terms. To this end, I want to begin our discussion of depression by emphasizing what it is *not*, namely, a temporary feeling of sadness resulting from any number of losses, such as those discussed in Chapter 3. Regrettably, some people seem to confuse sadness with depression, and because treating a condition we don't really have can be both costly and dangerous, it is vital to keep the distinction between a very natural reaction to "life's downs" and an actual episode of depression in mind as you familiarize yourself with the nature and scope of this particular barrier to success.

Unlike a temporary bout of the blues, real depression is an illness that persists over time (usually two or more weeks) and is accompanied by a plethora of mental and physical symptoms. According to the Mayo Clinic (2012), these symptoms can include the following:

- Loss of interest and/or pleasure in formerly enjoyable activities
- An increase or decrease in all appetites, including those for sleep, food, and/or sex
- Weight gain or loss
- Fatigue, irritability, and/or anxiety
- Difficulty remembering or concentrating
- Low self-esteem
- Body aches
- Inexplicable crying spells or mood swings
- Thoughts of death or suicide.

As you can see, depression is far more than just feeling blue—it generally affects every aspect of your life from the time you get up in the morning to the time you go to bed at night. It affects how you feel about yourself, how you feel about everything in your life, and how you feel about your future. For this reason, it often leads to a host of other issues, including work or school problems, family conflicts, relationship difficulties, social isolation, suicide, and self-mutilation (Mayo, 2012).

Identifying the Problem: How Do I Know If I Truly Am Depressed?

Aside from the aforementioned symptoms that can, by the way, range from mild to severe, there are a number of other factors that *may* indicate that these particular symptoms are a result of depression, including a family history of this condition; being female; very high stress levels occasioned by specific events; traumatic childhood experiences; social isolation; addictions; certain medical conditions and/or medications; low self-esteem; and a tendency toward pessimism (Mayo, 2012). With regard to college students in particular, depression is likely to result in cigarette use, alcohol abuse (which may be followed by unsafe sex), and drug abuse (NIMH, 2011).

If, based upon your symptoms and your possible exposure to some of these other risk factors, you believe you may be suffering from depression—be it mild, moderate or severe—you should speak with a therapist or with your healthcare professional as a first step to obtaining a diagnosis and initiating a treatment plan. This first step is especially critical if you are having recurrent thoughts of suicide.

Understanding the Problem: What Causes Depression?

There are probably as many causes of depression as there are symptoms of the disease, all of which result from the interplay of biological, genetic and environmental factors (Mayo, 2012). On the biological side of the scale, certain "naturally occurring brain chemicals [known as neurotransmitters] are thought to play a direct role in depression" (Mayo, 2012). As you might guess from their name, neurotransmitters are simply the brain's messengers, and, as such, they control our mood, our biological desires (including those for sleep, food, and sex), and our propensity for positive or negative thinking. Though these chemical messengers are indeed very tiny, do not let their size fool you. They are enormously powerful determinants of thoughts, desires, and behaviors.

Depression can also be caused by hormonal problems, some of which have been well publicized. Two well publicized causes of depression include thyroid problems and menopause (Mayo, 2012), conditions that a simple blood test can detect. One less publicized cause of depression results from an insulin resistance that most people do not know they have. Simply put, if you are insulin resistant, it means that your body does not recognize and will not use its own insulin, the hormone that clears your blood of sugar. Thus, you develop an overabundance of insulin in your system which, in turn, affects your adrenal hormones (i.e., your cortisol levels) and your sex hormones (i.e., your estrogen, progesterone, and testosterone), regardless of whether you are male or female. All of these hormonal imbalances can lead to depression.

Other biological causes of depression include certain medications you may be taking, having a serious illness, some of the chemical addictions discussed in Chapter 4 (Mayo, 2012), and specific vitamin deficiencies (particularly the B vitamins).

But depression can have psychological causes as well, a number of which likewise affect the brain's neurotransmitter levels, most notably abuse and trauma. Other psychological factors that often interface with the biological include major losses and high stress. Additionally, while research in the area of technology and depression is ongoing, I have often thought that living in a society that has given us countless ways to keep in touch, technologically speaking, while simultaneously enabling us to remain physically isolated from one another may contribute to depression as well. Why? Because human beings need a fair amount of real human contact to feel truly connected and fulfilled. Put another way, we are social animals, and technology can actually be somewhat isolating, no matter how connected it ostensibly makes us feel.

Though often overlooked, environmentally caused stress is a particular concern for college students and would include "living away from family for the first time, missing family or friends, feeling alone or isolated, experiencing conflict in relationships, facing new and sometimes difficult school work, and worrying about finances" (NIMH, 2011).

As noted above, one final cause of depression is genetic. Research has shown that "depression is more common in people whose biological family members also have the condition" (Mayo, 2012), and researchers are currently "trying to find genes that may be involved in causing depression" (Mayo, 2012).

One critical point that I hope has emerged from the foregoing discussion is that, despite our societal messages to the contrary, depression is *not* your fault and is *not* something that you can control just by changing your attitude or outlook. It is a real medical condition, and, as such, it needs to be treated just like any other medical condition. The *good* news is that there are a number of highly effective treatments from which to choose.

Solving the Problem: Pathways to Healing Depression

The first step to overcoming any of the personal barriers discussed in this book is often the hardest one, namely, admitting that we may, in fact, have a problem. Our own pride or the feelings of shame or guilt that accompany these barriers often make it difficult for us to take that first step, but if we truly want to achieve our goals in life, there is no other choice for us to make. The second step requires that we take a holistic approach to healing by asking for help, on the one hand, and by learning to help ourselves on the other.

Asking for Help

When it comes to depression, you can ask both healthcare professionals and therapists who specialize in treating this condition for help, and once you do so, you will be given the following options from which to choose, depending upon the type of depression with which you may be diagnosed (e.g., major depression, dysthymia, seasonal affective disorder, or bipolar disorder).

Medication: The purpose of antidepressant medication is to restore the balance of your neurotransmitters, and many of these medications do so quite effectively, though they are not without side effects, all of which you should discuss with your healthcare professional. In addition, finding the right dose of the right antidepressant for you is a process of trial and error, and each one takes time to work, so you do need to be patient with this particular approach to treatment (Mayo, 2012). If your depression results from a thyroid condition or from an insulin resistance, however, you should begin to feel some relief fairly rapidly once these conditions are treated.

Counseling Therapy: If you think your depression may also result from the aforementioned psychological factors (i.e., abuse, trauma, stress, or loss), individual or group counseling therapy is also a very effective treatment option and can be used along with antidepressant medication or as an alternative to it. Like medications, counseling therapy serves to restore the balance of your brain's neurotransmitters; it just takes longer and is generally more expensive, though many therapists offer sliding fee scales. You may also have access to a therapist, free of charge, at your college's health center. One very effective form of therapy that is used to treat depression is known as Cognitive Behavioral Therapy or CBT for short (Mayo, 2012).

The premise behind CBT is very simple: your feelings result from your thoughts. In other words, by harboring negative thoughts, such as "I'm no good at math and never will be" or "I am too broken to ever heal and be happy," you can actually cause yourself to feel depressed. There are many different types of negative or pessimistic thought patterns that CBT will teach you to recognize and counter, and the benefits of so doing are both long lasting and fairly immediate.

Complementary Medicine: There are also a number of alternative treatments for mild to moderate depression, some of which include Inositol, St. John's Wort, SAM-E, certain vitamins and minerals, fish and flaxseed oils, homeopathy, acupuncture, meditation, massage therapy, and yoga – to name but a few. Some doctors are familiar with these complementary treatments, but many are not, so your best bet is to find someone who specializes in this area. Though herbal treatments are generally free of serious side effects, you should never try to self-medicate, especially because these herbs can sometimes interfere with other medications you may be taking or they may not be strong enough to meet your needs. For this reason, you should always speak with your healthcare professional before using complementary medicines (Mayo, 2012).

Other Medical Treatments: For more severe cases of depression, other treatments do exist and can be quite effective as well (e.g., electroconvulsive therapy, vagus nerve stimulation, transcranial magnetic stimulation or even a brief period of hospitalization), but again, these treatments are reserved for very stubborn or severe cases of depression (Mayo, 2012). Most people will benefit from one or more of the milder treatment plans discussed above. With regard to other medical treatments, do not forget to rule out conditions such as a thyroid dysfunction or an insulin resistance as part of your treatment plan. When it comes to depression, the key is to eliminate all possible causes so that you can target its most likely cause.

Learning to Help Yourself

If you wish to scale any of the personal barriers discussed in this book, asking for assistance is only half the battle. You must also learn to help yourself. With respect to depression, there are a number of very effective ways to beat the blues, all of which you can begin to implement and benefit from almost immediately.

> *Get Moving*: Daily vigorous exercise in the form of power walking, aerobics, swimming, jogging, and biking will help your depression by stimulating the release of other chemicals, known as endorphins, that positively affect mood as well. Weight lifting can likewise be a useful antidote to depression, primarily because it makes you look (and, therefore, feel) better and because the breathing and counting it necessitates can relieve the stress that also causes depression.

> *Get Connected:* One of the most troubling aspects of depression is that it causes most of us to isolate ourselves from others in much the same way any other illness does. Quite simply, when we don't feel well, we don't want to be around other people. Unfortunately, when it comes to depression, the more isolated we are, the worse it becomes. Thus, you absolutely must get (and stay) connected to other people and/or to pets, even if you really do not feel like it. You might want to begin by volunteering at one of your local community service organizations. You can find one that would be of interest to you by logging onto VolunteerMatch.org. Why volunteer? Aside from fostering the social connections that will help to

ameliorate your depression, it will also make you feel good about yourself, and feeling good about yourself will go a long way toward helping you to heal. Make a commitment to volunteering at least once a week and keep that commitment sacred. If you are struggling to do so, remember that, when treating depression, you will *only* feel the benefits of your actions *after* you initiate them—never before.

Watch What You Eat: Healthy eating is important when treating any medical condition, including depression. If you reduce or eliminate unhealthy foods from your diet, your depression may improve, not just because you are consuming more vitamins and minerals but because you may begin to look better as well (especially if your depression has caused you to gain weight) and looking better often makes people feel better. Try adopting a healthy diet for at least two weeks (without cheating). If you don't notice any improvement in your overall well-being, you need not stay on it, though you should still limit your intake of junk foods as well as alcohol (which is, by the way, a natural depressant). If you are insulin resistant, you will need to significantly limit your intake of sugary foods as well as those foods that rapidly convert to sugar.

Express Your Feelings: If you don't express the feelings you tend to ignore, repress, or deny, you may continue to suffer from depression. The more you hold inside, the worse it can make you feel. How you express your feelings is a matter of personal choice. You might wish to confront someone with whom you have a conflict, engage in some type of physical activity such as boxing or racquetball, or consistently write in a journal. If your depression is related to someone or something you have lost, please see Chapter 3 where you will find some useful coping strategies.

Get Your Z's:: There is a very high correlation between lack of sleep and depression, so much so that depression can both cause and result from sleep deprivation. This close connection may very well explain why insomnia is one of the first symptoms of depression to appear and one of the first to disappear once treatment begins.

Address Your Stress: There is likewise a strong correlation between high stress and depression, so if you are under a lot of stress right now, by all means skip ahead to Chapter 6 where you will find some very effective stress management techniques.

Take Control of Your Addictions: Depression and addictions go hand in hand, so if you are battling an addiction or an eating disorder, you may likewise want to skip ahead to Chapters 4 and 5 where you will find specific strategies to address these behaviors.

Think Positive: Every time you catch yourself thinking negatively, practice an informal version of CBT by countering that negative thought with its exact opposite and repeat this new positive thought to yourself several times until it feels more true to you than the negative thought once did. For example, using CBT, the statement that "I am too broken to heal" becomes "I am healing and with a little time and effort, I will definitely overcome the challenges I am currently facing." If you want to take this informal version of CBT one step further, wear a rubber band around your wrist and gently snap yourself every time you have a negative thought that you need to counter. Doing so will draw your attention to the frequency of these thoughts, thereby helping you to correct them every day. Also believe that you have what it takes to achieve your dreams because, quite simply, *you do*. Remember what Henry Ford said: "If you think you can or cannot do a thing, you're right." When you put the power of your mind to work for you rather than against you, you will be amazed at the results you can achieve. You have heard this truism before— you just haven't committed to it. If you are suffering from depression, *now* is the time to do so.

Read: Also known as "biblio-therapy," reading about depression and learning how others are coping with it can go a long way toward helping you feel better at the same time you may acquire some valuable techniques for healing.

Get in Touch With the Spiritual … Whatever That Means for You: Find that "higher power" that provides you with a sense of peace, calming, serenity, tranquility, strength, and renewal (be it prayer, nature walks, or artistic expressions) and spend a few minutes with it each day. When you begin to attend to your "spirit" in this way, however you interpret that, so, too, will you begin to heal your mind and your body. Incorporating some type of spirituality into the healing process is especially effective because it can help you begin to recognize that you are not a depressed person, but rather, a whole person for whom depression is temporarily present. It may take you awhile to grasp and really internalize this particular concept, but it's an important one to master so that you no longer feel flawed or damaged. Many things can come and go in our lives, including various symptoms of depression, but as we will discuss in Chapter 8, none of these things in any way defines who we truly are as human beings.

Take Care of Yourself: While I applaud those who spend their lives tending to the needs of others, I also know how high a price these same individuals can pay for this behavior in the form of depression and other such conditions if they completely neglect their own needs. This self-neglect can lead to a great deal of resentment which can, in turn, fuel depression. If you fall into this category, it is critical that you begin finding ways to nurture yourself every day. Maybe that means listening to soothing music, meditating, playing an instrument, spending time in nature, working on a hobby, reading a good book, walking your dog, exercising, or even taking a warm bath. It does not really matter what you do as long as it is a dedicated act of self-care, self-nurturing, and self-love.

Final Remarks

In the end, when it comes to overcoming depression, please remember that this condition is not your fault and that it really is highly treatable, even if the treatments take some time. Believe in the pathway(s) to healing you select, and you will most assuredly beat the blues once and for all—of this you can be absolutely certain.

2

When You Just Can't Fight Your Fear:

Understanding Anxiety

You have within you the power to obliterate many superfluous and disturbing things, for they are entirely in your mind.

--Marcus Aurelius

Use your fear. It will take you to places where you store your courage.

--Amelia Earhart

My first exposure to the prevalence of anxiety came to me as a young graduate student when I went to our local library to do some research on the subject and found that every single book—and there were many— had already been checked out. It was then that I began to understand just how widespread this particular barrier to success really is, an impression that has been repeatedly confirmed as I have witnessed the number of students who suffer from some form of anxiety. In fact, if I were to name one of the most common barriers to college success that I have personally observed, it would be none other than anxiety.

Defining the Problem: What is Anxiety?

As was the case with depression, for the sake of clarity, I am going to begin our discussion of anxiety with a definition of what it is not, namely, the perfectly normal fear or concern we all have when we are asked to perform a task for the first time (e.g., driving a car) or when we engage in any number of life's stress-inducing situations, such as taking an exam, giving a speech, asking someone out on a first date, running from danger, and so forth (NIMH, 2012). This perfectly normal fear or concern may likewise be accompanied by equally normal physical symptoms, such as a racing heartbeat, perspiration, and tremors.

In contrast, real anxiety is a state of mind that produces many of the aforementioned symptoms—both emotional and physical— but it does not go away and it is often excessive for a given situation. Characteristic of all types of anxiety is the inability to relax—be it all day every day or primarily when exposed to certain situations or objects (also known as "triggers"). The common denominator that often (but not always) characterizes anxiety is an accompanying addiction (NIMH, 2011) and/ or depression (Mayo, 2012.)

While there are many types of anxiety disorders, the following are among the most common:

Generalized Anxiety Disorder: According to the National Institute of Mental Health (2012), people with Generalized Anxiety Disorder (also known as GAD) are constantly worried or fearful—regardless of whether or not there is anything to be fearful or worried about. They are also far more likely to experience excessive anxiety over ordinary life events related to health, relationships, finances, school, and work (NIMH, 2012). The inability to relax that is intrinsic to GAD is often accompanied by a variety of physical symptoms, including restlessness; difficulty concentrating, sleeping, or swallowing; fatigue; headaches; muscle tension or aches; twitching or jerking; irritability; sweating; dizziness; breathlessness; frequent urination; and upset stomach (NIMH, 2012).

Both the excessive worry and the physical symptoms GAD invariably produces are what cause so many college students to struggle in school. Preparing for class, going to class, being in class, or doing homework for class can all serve to heighten their anxiety.

Panic Disorder: My students with panic disorder have described it in much the same way as it is defined by the National Institute of Mental Health (2012), namely, as a "sudden [attack] of terror, usually accompanied by a pounding heart, sweatiness, weakness, faintness or dizziness." At best, it may feel like a heart attack, a form of insanity, or a total loss of control, and, at worst, it may feel as though death is imminent (NIMH, 2012). It can happen anywhere at any time of the day or night, and it is this unpredictability, even more so than the aforementioned physical symptoms, that often interferes with a student's college life. A panic attack or a fear of one may prevent students from getting to class on time (if at all), it may cause them to leave class early, or it may cause them to fail to prepare for class adequately. According to my own students, the fear of when/where a panic attack may occur can be as distracting and as debilitating as the panic attack itself.

Obsessive Compulsive Disorder: Individuals who suffer from OCD use some type of repetitive behavior to quell their anxiety-provoking thoughts (NIMH, 2012). For example, I had a student who became so overwrought with anxiety every time she thought about how her peers and her instructor would review her rough drafts in her freshman composition class that she could not stop revising her essay drafts and would eventually drop her English courses before she ever had to submit a final draft. For this reason, she had to take her freshman composition course four times before she actually passed it. Other more classic examples of OCD include compulsive hand washing due to a fear of germs, repeatedly checking door locks due to a fear of robberies, and various forms of counting, touching, organizing and hoarding (NIMH, 2012). OCD's can affect a student's academic performance not just because they may be school-related but also because they can require a lot of time to maintain.

Post Traumatic Stress Disorder: Many people still associate PTSD with war veterans suffering from "shell shock," but it is actually a form of anxiety that can affect anyone who has experienced or witnessed any type of trauma, including child abuse, rape, car accidents, and natural disasters—to name but a few (NIMH, 2012). The symptoms of PTSD can include those associated with other anxiety disorders, but PTSD can be far more severe in the form of hypervigilence (i.e., always being alert to possible danger), aggressiveness, numbed feelings, loss of interest in formerly pleasurable activities, flashbacks, nightmares, and avoidance of circumstances related to the trauma (NIMH, 2012). As I have seen firsthand, these symptoms can most certainly have a negative impact on a student's academic performance, depending upon their severity. Most often, they prevent students from successfully completing their courses.

Phobic Disorders: People who suffer from phobic disorders experience intense fear when exposed to something that is highly unlikely to cause them any real harm (NIMH, 2012). Some of the most common phobias include fear of small spaces (claustrophobia), fear of heights (acrophobia), fear of flying, fear of needles, and fear of social situations (also known as Social Anxiety Disorder). Phobias affect college students the most when they relate to a certain career choice (e.g., the student who wants to pursue a career in medicine but is too afraid of needles or blood to do so) or when they relate to a specific subject, such as mathematics, the avoidance of which can significantly lengthen the time it may take a student to graduate. Other performance-based phobias, such as a fear of success, a fear of failure, or a fear of making the wrong choices can effectively sabotage a student's ability to complete his or her course of study.

Identifying the Problem: How Do I Know If I Have Anxiety?

There are two key differences between an anxiety disorder and the perfectly normal fears and concerns that we all experience at various times in our lives. First, anxiety does not go away on its own; in fact, a diagnosis is not made unless it has persisted for at least six months—and true anxiety tends to worsen over time (NIMH, 2012). Secondly, unlike normal fears and concerns, anxiety will often prevent us from taking some sort of action. For example, the average person may feel slight trepidation at the thought of flying 30,000 feet above the ground whereas the person who has claustrophobia or a fear of flying will avoid air travel altogether. So, if one or more of the aforementioned types of anxiety seems to apply to your situation, if it has persisted over time, if it has affected your behavior or your performance, and if any of the causes of anxiety described below likewise apply to you, you may, in fact, be suffering from an anxiety disorder. As was the case with depression, of course, the first step toward an accurate diagnosis is to consult a licensed mental health professional or your healthcare provider.

Understanding the Problem: What Causes Anxiety?

The causes of anxiety are almost identical to those of depression, probably because the two conditions are so closely related. Once again, there seems to be an interplay between biological, genetic, and environmental factors (NIMH, 2012). Biologically speaking, some of the same neurotransmitters that are implicated in depression are likewise thought to be responsible for anxiety. Additionally, using the latest advances in brain imaging technology, researchers have also been able to identify the parts of the brain that are most associated with anxiety—including that which stores the emotional memories that can lead to phobias and that which seems to grow smaller in response to traumatic experiences and events (NIMH, 2012). Finally, as was the case with depression, anxiety has also been linked to specific medical conditions as well as to medications such as antihistamines (Mayo, 2012).

With respect to genetics, a family history of anxiety may likewise cause certain individuals to develop this disorder (Mayo, 2012), not just because of heredity, however, but also because, as Judith Orloff (2009) points out in her book <u>Emotional Freedom</u>, anxiety can be a "learned response" from one's parents. The old adage "apples don't fall far from the tree" is quite true with regard to the genes we inherit from our parents as well as from the behaviors they model for us.

With regard to the environmental factors that are associated with anxiety, there are a number of life experiences that may cause an individual to develop an anxiety disorder, including childhood abuse, major traumas, high levels of stress (Mayo, 2012) and a frightful experience with a potential trigger (e.g., a particularly turbulent flight that gives rise to a fear of flying).

Solving the Problem: Pathways to Healing Anxiety

Once you have identified anxiety as one of your personal barriers to success in college (and perhaps in life), you will derive the most benefit from adopting the holistic approach to healing described in Chapter 1, especially because, as noted earlier, depression and anxiety are so closely related.

Asking for Help

If you speak to your healthcare provider or to a mental health professional as a first step to healing your anxiety, you will find that your options will be similar to those that are used to treat depression. Each one is described below.

> *Medication:* A number of medications are used to manage anxiety disorders once other medical causes have been ruled out, but the three most common are benzodiazepines, antidepressants, and beta blockers (NIMH, 2012). Benzodiazepines work fairly quickly, but they are addictive and they tend to lose their effectiveness over time, thus necessitating progressively higher

doses to achieve the same result. For this reason, together with the fact that they can cause unpleasant withdrawal symptoms, it is best to use them for short periods of time—if at all (NIMH, 2012). The real danger with habit-forming drugs and anxiety disorders, of course, is that some individuals with anxiety may also be prone to addictions, so introducing them to a substance that could potentially lead them to develop a primary or secondary addiction might not be in their best interest. Finally, as with all drugs, benzodiazepines can also have unpleasant side effects, most notably drowsiness or dizziness. Antidepressant medications are likewise used to treat anxiety disorders primarily because they adjust the balance of the same neurotransmitters that are responsible for both conditions. Though they, too, are not without side effects, and though they may take awhile to work, they are a much safer choice because they are not habit forming. Lastly, beta blockers, a class of drugs most often used to treat specific cardiovascular conditions such as irregular heartbeats, may be prescribed to reduce the physical symptoms of certain anxiety disorders (NIMH, 2012).

Counseling Therapy: Mental health professionals use a number of different techniques to treat anxiety disorders, but two of the most common are **Cognitive Behavioral Therapy** and **Systematic Desensitization.** As was the case with depression, when it comes to anxiety, we can literally "think ourselves sick" in much the same way we can make ourselves sick by not eating well, exercising regularly, or getting enough sleep. The mind is a very powerful tool when it comes to causing or controlling anxiety. The more anxious thoughts we have (e.g., "I'll never pass Professor Martin's class" or "I am probably going to get fired for this," or "I won't be able to survive this break up"), the higher our anxiety levels as well as their accompanying physical symptoms. If you don't believe me, try it out for yourself: Think about the worst thing you can imagine happening in your life right now actually occurring and see if you don't feel something change in your stomach or your heart or your body temperature or any one of your physical expressions. Even a twitching eyelid counts. Given the close relationship between our thoughts and our reactions to them, it stands to reason that if we can think ourselves sick, then we can think ourselves well too, and that is where Cognitive Behavioral Therapy has been shown to be very effective in the treatment of anxiety. It's all about retraining our minds to produce rational, calming thoughts rather than irrational, fear-producing ones. Again, you can try it out for yourself by taking an anxiety provoking thought such as "I'll never pass Professor Martin's class" and transforming it into a calming thought such as "I will pass Professor Martin's class because I have the ability, the time, and the determination that it takes to do so, and even if I don't pass it, it's not the end of the world. I will seek the help I need to pass it the second time around." As you practice CBT techniques with your therapist, not only will you learn to control your anxious thoughts but so, too, will you control the physical symptoms that they so often produce.

Systematic Desensitization is primarily used for anxiety disorders that relate to specific fears and phobias. The premise behind this therapeutic approach is quite simple and once again involves the power of the mind: Simply put, we tend to enlarge our fears with our thoughts (or our catastrophic imaginings) about them. So, for example, we don't imagine a simple airplane ride … we imagine feeling trapped, unable to breathe, having a panic attack, or even dying in a plane crash. Thus, we avoid that which we fear. Systematic Desensitization causes us to lessen our fears by deliberately exposing us to the feared object or experience in small doses so that we get used to it, and it no longer has any power over us. We might, for example, begin with some guided visualizations wherein we imagine ourselves buying a plane ticket, packing our suitcases, driving to the airport, checking in, walking up the ramp, boarding the plane, taking off, actually making it though the flight, and disembarking —all without incident. From there, we could take small steps to act out our guided visualizations until airplanes are no longer a source of extreme fear. In the end, we will come to see that whatever it is we feared might happen does not actually occur and this rational knowledge will, in turn, supplant our irrational fears.

Aside from specific types of therapy such as Cognitive Behavioral Therapy or Systematic Desensitization, some anxiety disorders also respond well to traditional "talk therapy," and that is because, as noted in Chapter 1, talk therapy likewise works to rebalance the brain's neurotransmitters in much the same way as certain medications do.

Alternative Treatments: A number of alternative medicines are used to treat mild to moderate anxiety, including Inositol (also used for depression), GABA (Gamma Aminobutyric Acid), and a variety of herbs, but it is always best to discuss the use and proper dosage with a licensed healthcare professional to ensure that your particular needs are being safely met. This type of complementary medicine, for example, would not be sufficient to treat an anxiety disorder that is accompanied by other issues such as an addiction or self-mutilating behavior. Other complementary treatments include yoga, acupuncture, homeopathy, massage therapy, and meditation (see below).

Learning to Help Yourself

At the same time you are seeking professional assistance for your anxiety disorder, you can also help yourself by applying the healing strategies I discuss below, some of which also appear in Chapter 1.

> *Exercise:* As was the case with depression, there are two types of physical activity that may benefit those of you who suffer from anxiety. Movement that involves breathing and counting (such as yoga and weight lifting) can be very calming as can aerobic exercise since it releases those "feel good" chemicals known as endorphins that are likewise enormously calming. Exercise will only help you combat your anxiety if you commit to it, however, so it is best to make it part of your daily routine.

> *Establish Daily Routines:* If you suffer from anxiety, you may not like unplanned events since these types of unforeseen activities can give rise to your feelings of not being in control, and these same feelings may heighten your anxiety levels. Thus, having set daily routines can provide you with a sense of stability and security at the same time they can serve to distract you from whatever it is that is causing you to feel anxious, especially if you make a conscious effort to concentrate on the task at hand rather than letting your mind wander down dark corridors of fear. If necessary, you can do as certain practitioners of meditation do to ground themselves in the present moment and actually talk yourself through a routine so that you stay focused on it. For example, when washing dishes, you could say, "I am turning on the hot water, I am adding soap to the water, I am lifting this plate off the counter," and so forth. Your mind cannot hold two thoughts at the same time, so your anxious thoughts will fade into the background while you deliberately focus your attention on whatever activity you are completing.

Create Healthy Distractions: This healing strategy is a special kind of routine, though you may or may not choose to engage in it daily. The idea is to create something that will serve to calm and pleasantly distract you. Your potential creations are limited only by your imagination. Do you, for example, like to—or would you like to—paint, draw, sing, dance, garden, cook, write, sculpt, act, photograph scenes from nature, or design flower arrangements? Talent is irrelevant when it comes to managing your anxiety in this way. All that matters is that the process of creating is something you enjoy doing and something that completely captures your attention while you are doing it. An alternative to creating a product is to develop a hobby such as chess, stamp collecting, horseback riding, an athletic activity, and so forth—again, something you enjoy doing or would enjoy doing and something that you will find distracting. The main reason creating healthy distractions is so important is because it is based upon a fact of life: whatever we attend to expands. In other words, the more we focus on something, the larger it becomes until, in some instances, it eventually consumes us. When we turn our attention to something else, that which we turn from (e.g., the source of our anxiety) loses some of its intensity and power.

Breathe: Yes, you can do it very effectively through a plethora of proven meditation techniques (or prayerful meditation if you are so inclined), but don't discount what I call the "simple act of breathing." Every so often, when your anxiety really flairs up, just stop and take a few very slow and deep breaths from your abdomen, not from your chest. If you wish, you can say something like "peace" with each inhalation, but the breathing alone should have a fairly powerful effect on you. Commit these words —just breathe—to memory and use them as often as needed.

Spend Time With Nature: Few people realize just how calming nature can be until they spend some time outdoors in a place of natural beauty. For you, it might be the beach while for another, it might be a mountain hike. The setting is not nearly as important as its effect on you. There is something about gazing up at the stars or out upon the ocean or down a mountain peak that is profoundly calming and that often serves in some strange way to put our troubles in perspective. Since high levels of noise can aggravate anxiety, an added benefit of spending time in nature is that it will provide you with a quiet environment as well. Try it and see if it does not prove to have a very calming effect on you.

Stay Connected: Anxiety thrives on loneliness and is often at its worst when you are alone with your thoughts, so make it a point to get (or to stay) connected with people and/or pets. As mentioned in Chapter 1, you could begin by volunteering at one of your local community service organizations. Not only does volunteer work keep you connected to others but it can also serve to distract you from your anxiety. If you suffer from social anxiety, you may want to start by connecting with a pet and move on to people once you learn to manage your condition.

Get In Touch With Your Senses: Believe it or not, our bodies can have an enormously calming effect on our minds if we stimulate our five senses, a point that Claudia Strauss (2004) makes very well in her book <u>Talking to Anxiety</u>. In it, she discusses a number of ways to use the body to calm the mind. For example, the sense of touch to calm anxiety might include getting a therapeutic massage, soaking in a warm bath, sitting in a rocking chair, stroking a pet, or feeling the heat of a warm blanket, a heating pad or a fire in the fireplace. The sense of taste might include a cup of Chamomile tea or a warm bowl of Chicken Noodle Soup. The sense of smell could include lavender or vanilla candles or lotions. The sense of hearing might include soothing music, particularly something you have not heard before, such as classical music, which can have a calming effect on people of all ages—from infants to centurions. Or, you might buy a CD that simulates the sounds of nature (e.g., a quiet rainfall, the ebb and flow of the surf, or gentle winds). Finally, the sense of sight might include watching the fish in your aquarium (if you have one) or the waves on the beach. All of these sense activities tend to slow your breathing and lower your heart rate at the same time they can calm your mind.

Get Enough Rest: Lack of sleep can affect the neurotransmitters that cause depression and anxiety, so it is important not to deny yourself the amount of sleep you need to feel fully rested. As noted earlier, both depression and anxiety can disturb your sleep, so if you are having trouble sleeping, you should speak with your healthcare provider.

Beware of Unhealthy Distractions: One of the ways individuals with anxiety disorders may seek relief is by developing addictions. While this topic is addressed at some length in Chapter 4, for now, I want to caution you to be very careful not to develop a dependency on anything, including one or more of the aforementioned healing strategies, to cope with your anxiety. It would be very easy, for example, to allow the use of certain comfort foods to escalate into a full blown food addiction. If you suspect that you are using an addiction to relieve your anxiety, please see Chapter 4.

Watch What You Ingest: Remember that certain substances, such as caffeine, nicotine, and alcohol can aggravate your anxiety, so it is best to avoid them (Mayo, 2012). In addition, as was the case with depression, it is likewise best for individuals with anxiety to "avoid fatty, sugary and processed foods" and to instead consume "vegetables, fruits, whole grains, and fish" (Mayo, 2012). If you are diagnosed with Generalized Anxiety Disorder, it is especially important to "include foods in your diet that are rich in omega-3 fatty acids and B vitamins" (Mayo, 2011). Finally, you may also wish to speak to your doctor about any medications you are taking or that you plan to take since they, too, can worsen your anxiety levels. The same is true of illegal substances (Mayo, 2012).

Final Remarks

When I was in graduate school, I remember one of my counseling professors describing anxiety as a "thief that robs us of our *joie de vivre*"—that is, the joy of living—and I found myself readily agreeing with him. Indeed, how can anyone who is haunted by fear possibly experience true joy? What saddens me more than the presence of this thief in the lives of my students, however, is that so many of them are not aware that, like its cousin depression, anxiety is a very treatable condition, a fact that is quite evident when we stop to really consider that we are not the fear based thoughts that seem to control us. We are so much more than that, and it is the recognition and acceptance of this very fact that will go a long way toward helping us heal the anxiety disorder(s) from which we suffer. It is at this point that we will discover the hidden benefit hiding behind our hidden barrier —a joy such that we have never known before, a joy that can completely transform our lives.

3

When You Just Need to Cry:

Understanding Grief and Loss

Suffering is not an elective; it's a core course in the university of life.
--Steven J. Lawson

All I know from my own experience is that the more loss we feel, the more grateful we should be for whatever it was we had to love. It means that we had something worth grieving for. I'm sorry for the ones that go through life not knowing what grief is.
--Frank O'Connor

What images come to mind when you hear the words "grief" or "grieving"? If you thought of someone you have personally lost, such as a parent, a sibling, or a friend, or if you thought of someone our nation has lost, such as Martin Luther King Jr., you are not alone. Most people associate the word "grief" with death, and that may well explain why it frequently becomes a hidden barrier to college success for so many students. While it is true that these same students may, in fact, have lost a loved one, it is equally true that they have not yet learned to identify the many other types of loss they experience. As a result, they have not been able to grieve (i.e., properly resolve) their losses, and their declining grade point average is often the unfortunate consequence. It is, therefore, my intent to use this chapter to help you learn to recognize the many faces of grief in your life and to provide you with some concrete strategies for addressing them.

Defining the Problem: What Is Grief/Loss?

Simply put, grief is a process that we all undergo when we lose someone or something we hold dear. As you can see from this definition, it includes more than just the loss of a loved one. It includes the loss of the future you will never have with that person and it includes the loss of anything that might be of value to you, such as a job, your health, a family heirloom, your home, a relationship, your appearance as you age or if you suffer a disfiguring injury, your faith in someone or something, your mobility, or even a dream that never came true (e.g., a close relationship with your now deceased parent). Grief may not always result from a present loss, however. Countless people have had to grieve unresolved losses from the past once they begin therapy.

All of these losses, past or present, cause us to experience grief—whether or not we are consciously aware of them as actual losses. College students, in particular, often do not realize how much loss is involved in leaving home or in graduating or transferring until it is upon them. Once they do so, they begin to acknowledge the sadness they feel. I have personally counseled a number of students who feel a real sense of loss when transferring from a community college to a university. Yes, they are excited about moving one step closer to their degree, but they are also sad to be leaving their teachers, their classmates, and even their campus behind. What they must come to understand, of course, is that every change in life will be accompanied by a sense of loss—even if the change is a good one (e.g., a wedding or a graduation).

Equally important, however, is the understanding that the grief they experience is a process, not a brief experience of one particularly salient emotion, such as sadness. There are many different facets of each person's grief process, and no two processes are exactly the same, despite what you may have heard about the stages of grief, ranging from denial to acceptance. These stages provide us with an academic understanding of grief, of course, but to really comprehend each person's grief process, I think it may be more helpful to think of grief as a period of time during which we will experience a number of changes in our emotions, in our perceptions, and, perhaps, in our belief systems as well

Identifying the Problem: How Do I Know If I Am Grieving?

There are many ways grief manifests itself within us—though not everyone will experience all of these reactions to loss. What follows are some of the words I have heard from individuals who have experienced the many faces of grief about which I am writing. They describe it this way:

Sad … so incredibly sad.
Like I don't know how I will go on without him (or her or it).
Like I don't know what to do now. Everything has changed.
Confused and lost … totally lost.
Angry … very, very angry.
Like I'm going crazy.
Hopeless.
Really hurt.
Lonely all the time.
Terrified. Exhausted. Empty. Numb. Disillusioned.
Afraid to try again.
Afraid to love again.

If I were to add to their thoughts, I would say that grief can also feel like a part (or all) of the solid ground upon which we were standing has been pulled out from under our feet. It is, by its very nature, an experience of insecurity and powerlessness. Something we loved, something we trusted, or something we depended upon for our support or even our sense of well-being is no longer there or is no longer there in the way that it once was, and there is absolutely nothing we can do to get it back. The primary loss of that something, ranging from a loved one to a deeply held belief, causes us to feel a secondary loss, namely, our sense of security or control in the world and that, in turn, adds to our feelings of confusion and even anger. Finally, as the comments above suggest, we may also "feel grief" in the form of depression or anxiety—or both.

It goes without saying, though I am going to say it anyway, that grief is an emotional experience more so than a physical one, though it can certainly include physical symptoms, such as insomnia or an upset stomach. In this case, however, our emotions are causing our physical symptoms. The emotional nature of grief is why it is so important to acknowledge and express whatever grief feels like for you—regardless of your culture, your age, or your gender. If you do not do so, your unresolved grief will manifest itself in a number of very destructive ways. In fact, just as grief has many faces, so, too, does unresolved grief. Also known as complicated grief, it may appear in the form of an addiction, depression, suicidal thoughts or behaviors, medical conditions such as heart disease, cancer and high blood pressure, anxiety (inclusive of PTSD), and drug or cigarette use or abuse (Mayo, 2011). When it comes to the loss of a loved one, in particular, complicated grief is characterized by a number of specific symptoms, including an inability to focus on anything save for the death of the one we loved; an unremitting longing for the loved one; a lack of acceptance of the death; feeling as though there is nothing left to live for and/or having thoughts of suicide; and feeling extreme guilt, self blame, bitterness, depression or anxiety—inclusive of social withdrawal (Mayo, 2011).

Complicated grief may also be more likely to result in individuals who have lost someone to suicide, who do not have a strong support system, or who do not adapt well to change (Mayo, 2011). They may likewise have had an "extremely close or dependent relationship" with the individual they lost or they were very ill prepared for the death (Mayo, 2011).

Because grief is an emotional process, individuals who are cut off from their own feelings, perhaps as a result of childhood abuse or trauma, may also be more likely to suffer from complicated grief. For them, it is simply too painful to feel anything at all and so they distance themselves from their own pain.

Understanding the Problem: How Do I Know If I Have Resolved My Grief?

I normally devote this part of each chapter to a discussion of cause, but since the cause of grief is self-evident (i.e., a significant loss), I thought it might be more helpful to spend some time discussing what happens when we successfully resolve our grief. Because grief is a process, not a one-time, one-emotion experience, you will move in and out of it even if years have passed since you first experienced the loss, most especially when you are exposed to certain "triggers" such as a song, a smell, a taste, or the sight of something that serves as a reminder of what was lost.

Despite the ongoing nature of the grief process, however, there are certain benchmarks that signal its resolution insofar as it can be "resolved." Remember: when you've lost someone or something, you will *always* feel the loss when you think about it or are reminded of it, but you will know that you have resolved it if you are no longer exclusively focused on that which was lost and if you are not controlled by the feelings your loss generated. Simply put, you will never be happy about your loss, but you will be at peace with it.

At this point in our discussion, I have no doubt that quite a few of you would like an answer to the question that is, in all likelihood, uppermost in your mind, namely, "How long will it take to resolve my grief?" You will probably not like my answer to this question, especially because those of you reading this book have grown up in a world of instant results—from microwaving your food to text messaging your best friend. When it comes to the resolution of grief, however, there are no "instants." In all honesty, I have absolutely no idea how long it will take for you to resolve your grief. It is different for everyone and is affected by a variety of factors, including your temperament, your life experiences, and the nature of your loss. Again, we are talking about a process, and every process takes time. Rather than focusing on the length of time it takes, try focusing on the healing strategies you can employ to complete the process successfully and meaningfully—always with the attitude that "it takes as long as it takes."

Solving the Problem: Pathways to Healing Grief

Because grief is both shared and personal, it is important to honor both aspects of the process by asking for help from others and by learning to help yourself during this difficult period of time.

Asking For Help

There are a number of ways to seek support as you work through your loss, including counseling, support groups, and family/community resources. Each is discussed below.

> *Grief Counseling:* Many people think that grief counseling should be reserved for individuals suffering from complicated grief, but I believe there are a number of reasons to see a mental health professional who specializes in grief and loss—even if you are not experiencing complicated grief. Grief counseling will allow you to spend some time in a supportive setting with someone who really understands the grieving process. In this very safe and confidential environment, you can reveal your most private thoughts about your loss, make sense of whatever you are feeling, benefit from a number of therapeutic techniques that will be suggested to you, and prepare to face your new future—whatever that may look like for you. One

other advantage of seeking therapeutic support for grief is that you will have the opportunity to resolve some of the other losses that your current loss may have stirred up for you. Such is the nature of the grief process—every new loss you suffer will, to an extent, resurrect those losses you thought you had resolved. So, even if you've never sought the help of a therapist before, do not discount the possibility of doing so now.

Support Groups: As noted above, grief is both shared and personal. There is a time to come together as a community of mourners and there is a time to close one's door to the world and face the silence that confirms that something we cherished is now gone. Grief and loss support groups speak to the shared aspect of the grief process. We need to share our grief with others because their emotional and physical support is what will allow us to begin healing. We also need to see that, despite our loss, we are *not* alone. Others are undergoing a similar process and they, too, are healing just as we will heal. In addition, like counseling therapy, grief and loss support groups can also provide us with a number of useful coping strategies.

Other Community Support: If you are grieving, this is the time to seek support from your family, your friends, and/or your spiritual community (if you have one). In fact, your ability to do so may be the single most important step you can take to begin healing. Many people feel some discomfort with the subjects of grief, loss, and death, but that does not mean that they do not wish to help someone they know who is suffering from a loss. Quite the contrary—they very much wish to help, but they may not always know how to best assist you, so do not be afraid to ask them for what you need. Sometimes it may be a hug; other times it may be a sympathetic ear or their presence during a particularly difficult time (such as an anniversary date). You will be amazed at how much support is just a simple request away … if you are not afraid to ask for it.

Learning to Help Yourself

As you work your way through your grief, you will undoubtedly discover ways to help yourself, but you may also find many of the following techniques quite useful as well.

> *Honor Your Routines:* As noted above, grief can leave you feeling very insecure and powerless, and this is why it is so important to adhere to the daily routines you followed before you suffered your loss. These routines include when you eat (even if you don't feel hungry), when you go to work and school, when you sleep (even if you have difficulty doing so for awhile), when you socialize (even if you'd rather be alone), and so forth. Such routines will provide you with some comfort, normality, and stability during the times you feel as though the sense of security you once felt in the world is gone forever.

> *Express Your Grief:* I could probably write another entire book about ways to express grief, but for our purposes, I will confine my remarks to two simple statements. First, you absolutely must express your grief if you want to resolve it successfully, and second, you need to find the manner of expression that works best for you. Do you need to write, paint, draw, dance, punch, sculpt, hike, run, talk, cry, or kick your way through your grief via any number of artistic, athletic, or therapeutic activities? In other words, how do *you* best express your feelings? When you feel angry, you may wish to physically express your anger on the racquetball court. When you feel sad, you may need to cry— alone or with someone else. When you feel lost and confused, you may need to write about what is most troubling to you. Many

people find it very useful to keep a grief journal. I did so when my sister died and found it enormously helpful to write about a number of different topics, including my favorite memories with her, what I would miss, what I regretted, what would never be, what I was feeling, what I needed, what she said that I wanted to remember, what I hoped for the future, and what I learned. If you lost a loved one, you may also choose to write a series of letters to that person. This technique is especially helpful if you have "unfinished business" with that individual or if you did not have a chance to say goodbye. If you'd rather not write, maybe you need to find a quiet place to talk to the one you have lost with the belief that what you say will somehow be heard. If you are artistically inclined, you may find it helpful to create a memory book or a collage that expresses what you have lost but will always treasure. Your manner of expressing your feelings is limitless ... experiment with different forms of emotional expression as you experience different feelings and see what works for you. The only "mistake" you can make in this process is to bury your feelings deep down inside rather than finding a way to release them.

Make Time for Grief: It has often been said that we make time for what is important to us, and if you have suffered a significant loss, there is absolutely nothing more important than making time for grief ... even though you would rather not do so. In fact, your aversion to giving grief the time it requires may keep you very, very busy— watching TV, working, developing an addiction, or socializing—to name but a few of the grief avoidance activities you might pursue. Each one serves to distract you from your grief, to deny its importance, and to prevent you from dealing with it. I have already discussed the dangers of avoiding your grief, but I have not yet provided you with an antidote for it, so here it is in a nutshell: Give yourself at least 20 minutes every day at a time and in a place you designate to be alone with your grief, to acknowledge the pain and/or to express it in a way that is healing for you. To avoid making time for grief only delays and exacerbates the inevitable. During this very painful time, make grieving your friend, albeit a rather disquieting friend, rather than your foe and give it the time it most assuredly deserves.

Comfort Yourself: There will be many people to comfort you once they learn of your loss, but you also need to comfort yourself, especially when you are alone with your grief. Self-comfort includes speaking gentle words of encouragement to yourself, such as: "Do not feel badly about feeling badly right now. This is a very normal reaction to loss." It can also include some of the same techniques individuals use to calm their anxiety, such as warm baths and warm cups of tea or soup, spending time in nature, working on a hobby or another pleasant distraction you enjoy, listening to soothing music, getting a massage or a manicure, buying yourself something special, and so forth. The point is to not neglect yourself, your needs, or your enjoyments just because you are grieving. You are essentially the same self you were before your loss and that self still needs your care and concern—especially during this very sad time.

Keep Moving: Part of taking care of yourself means taking care of your body, and there is perhaps no better way to do so than to exercise. In previous chapters, I discussed the benefits of exercise with regard to healing depression and anxiety, but it is equally beneficial for those who are grieving. Not only does it get you out of your house or apartment where you may feel overwhelmed by your loss but it also helps to relieve the intense stress that grief will almost always cause you to experience. The endorphins that are released with exercise will likewise help you to feel better. On a final but equally important note, exercise can become for you one of the daily routines that will restore a sense of stability and normality to your life.

Prepare for Grief Triggers: The first year following a significant loss may be the hardest one for you, though many people have stated that the second year is even harder. What makes these early years so difficult are the reminders that cannot be avoided. Such reminders include special dates or holidays, established traditions, or even daily routines (such as walking a beloved pet). All of these reminders can stir up painful feelings (Mayo, 2012) that are unavoidable, so it is very important to prepare for them ahead of time. To do so, you will need to create replacement activities and/or start new traditions. For example, if you used to spend New Year's Eve with your now deceased brother, you may wish to plan a weekend trip to the mountains with some friends. Or, if you used to have dinner with your ex-boyfriend every Friday night, you may wish to volunteer at a local community service organization that night instead. Part of taking care of yourself while also honoring your grief process is to prepare for those moments that are likely to intensify the pain you are feeling or have been feeling. Being prepared in this manner will go a long way toward helping you heal your grief.

Read: There are a number of wonderful books written by individuals who truly understand the grief process, books that can benefit you in two very important ways: First, like support groups, they will help you see that you are not alone (or crazy) as you respond to your loss and second, they will provide you with a lot of information to help you understand your unique grief process at the same time they will teach you about some excellent coping strategies, a number of which are tailored to specific types of losses.

Avoid Making Major Changes…For Awhile: Change is dangerous to someone who is grieving for three reasons: First, it can serve as an avoidance mechanism because it can keep us very busy … planning a wedding, moving into a new house, preparing for a new career, starting a new relationship, or giving birth to a child. Second, no one who has experienced a significant loss is in the right frame of mind to make a life-changing— and often irreversible—decision. And, finally, change is, by its very nature, unsettling and as much as possible, the grieving person needs a life that feels stable and settled. In the face of grief, the temptation to make major life changes is often enormous, but that is because we are looking for something—anything—to distract us from the intense pain we feel and to fill the emptiness that nothing and no one can fill for us—not a new home, not a new job, not a new relationship, and not a new baby. There is no easy or gentle way to say it: We must live with the pain until it eases. Then and only then will we be able to make informed, positive, life-altering decisions.

Look for the Lessons: It has been said that there is no greater teacher than adversity, and when it comes to grief and loss, truer words were never spoken. There is always something to be learned from loss. We may not want to learn these lessons in quite so painful a way, but identifying what we have learned can, in fact, be enormously healing. Very often, these lessons likewise serve as catalysts for personal growth, and the recognition of this fact can be equally healing. I recommend writing about what you have learned from your losses and periodically reviewing what you've written to reflect upon how these lessons have helped you to grow. To assist you in this regard, you might find it useful to answer questions such as: What do I know now that I did not know six to twelve months ago? How will my life change now that what I have lost is gone? What would I have done differently if given the chance and how will my answer to that question shape my future? As you consider these questions, you will undoubtedly find that your answers to them will range from the very simple to the deeply profound. There is no need to judge your responses, however. Whatever you learned from your experience of loss, whether simple or profound or some combination of the two, will move you one step closer to resolving your grief.

Final Remarks

As someone who has herself experienced grief and as someone who has spoken with countless individuals who have likewise suffered a variety of losses, I know that any words of comfort I might offer you by way of a closing remark are painfully inadequate. What I would like to share with you at this point, however, is that the resolution that concludes all grief processes might best be described by the words "three steps forward, two steps back." The three steps forward are most evident when we once again feel comfort, peace, love, and joy ... despite our loss. The two steps backward occur when we find ourselves deeply missing what we have lost. Because we are all unique, it is impossible for me to say how long or short these experiences of forward or backward movement may be, but what I can say with absolute certainty is that if we have truly resolved our grief, we will definitely experience more forward movements, though the backward ones may not completely disappear. In short, moving forward while sometimes looking back is part and parcel of the grief journey we all must make as we periodically heal from the many faces of grief we will most certainly encounter throughout our lives.

4

When You Just Can't Stop:

Understanding Addictions

*Habit may be likened to a cable; every day we
weave a thread, and soon we cannot break it.*
--Anonymous

Suffering isn't ennobling; recovering is.
--Christiann Barnard

Have you ever found yourself making any of the following statements?

"I can stop anytime I want to."
"I don't have a problem with this."
"Everybody does it."
"I am going to do this one last time, but it really is the last time—I swear."
"I deserve this because of how much I accomplished today."
"I deserve this because of how much I have suffered."

If you answered "yes" to the foregoing question—and even if you didn't— you may be one of the millions of people suffering from an addiction to something that is preventing you from reaching your full potential. Many of these same individuals do not recognize they have an addiction because they associate this word with alcohol or drugs. But, as you will learn in this chapter, virtually *anything* can become an addiction, and the point is to recognize your addictions so that you can control them. Until you do so, they will control you, thereby sabotaging your attempts to achieve success in college … and in life. Why? Because addictions almost always consume three of your most precious resources: your time, your energy, and your attention.

Defining the Problem: What Is An Addiction?

There are perhaps as many definitions of addictions as there are addictions themselves, almost all of which are expressed in the kind of clinical language that I am trying to avoid in this book. So, for our purposes, my non-clinical definition of an addiction is a behavior that has become a compulsive habit upon which someone is psychologically dependent. To expand on this definition somewhat, I would group addictions into two categories: those I call mild to moderate and those I call severe. Mild to moderate addictions do not always cause us serious physical harm, but they nonetheless require our time, our energy and our attention, thereby preventing us from reaching our potential at the same time they significantly affect the quality of our life. Mild to moderate addictions might include, for example, spending too much time working, exercising, daydreaming, watching TV, texting, or surfing the Internet (inclusive of face booking, blogging, or twittering). With regard to the latter, mild to moderate addictions related to the computer or hand-held electronic devices have become particularly problematic for college students and are just now being studied. Severe addictions likewise rob us of our precious resources but they are also much more likely to cause us serious physical or financial harm. This type of addiction would include using drugs or alcohol, smoking, gambling, over or under eating (inclusive of dieting), shopping, self-mutilation, pornography, and sex—to name but a few.

The common denominator that binds all addictive behavior is its essential purpose: to help us avoid something we would rather not face or feel (e.g., painful feelings, stress, or anxiety); something we think we cannot handle; or something we do not know how to handle. Every addiction, regardless of type, is a way to "check out" of life for as long as we desire … a few minutes, a few hours, a few days, or even for a lifetime. As Suzanne Somers (1999) points out in her book 365 Ways to Change Your Life, these addictions are never about thirst or hunger or material needs; they are merely a pleasure-producing distraction we have created to anesthetize ourselves. As such, they constitute a very unhealthy—and oftentimes potentially dangerous— coping mechanism that we would do well to eliminate if we truly wish to reach our potential and live a full and deeply satisfying life. The other common denominators binding all addictions are their obsessive compulsive nature, the loss of control they cause us to experience, and their essential power over us, no matter how great the cost—personally and/or professionally.

Identifying the Problem: How Do I Know If I Have An Addiction?

At the risk of minimizing the serious nature of this question, I am tempted to answer it on a humorous note by stating that *"Everyone* is addicted to *something."* My intent in so doing is not to make light of this topic but rather to underscore the widespread nature of addictive behavior so that, as you read through this section, you will not experience an inordinate degree of the two primary emotions that addictive behaviors so often cause us to feel, namely, guilt and shame. As is the case with every other personal barrier to college success discussed in this book, if you *do* suffer from an addictive behavior, you are definitely *not* alone. In fact, many people first develop addictions in college when they are faced with the stress of being on their own for the first time or having to juggle multiple responsibilities. College life also tends to expose students to potentially addictive substances like alcohol. Regardless of when or how your addiction started, however, the point is not to condemn yourself for having it but to acknowledge and heal whatever has caused it.

So, what exactly determines whether a person's behavior can be classified as an addiction? The American Psychiatric Association has identified certain key characteristics that indicate whether or not a person has an addiction to alcohol or drugs, but many of these same characteristics are applicable to other kinds of addictions. To this end, if you can answer "yes" to some of the following questions, you may, in fact, have an addiction:

- Does the activity or substance cause you to feel pleasure and does it alter your emotions or your mood?
- Have you increased the amount of the substance or the frequency of the activity over time?
- If you tried to stop using the substance or engaging in the activity, did you experience withdrawal symptoms in the form of irritability, anxiety, depression, nausea, vomiting, shaking, or other unpleasant physical reactions?
- Has the substance or activity harmed you in any way? For example, has it caused you to neglect your responsibilities at home, school, or work or has it created problems for you legally, socially, personally, or interpersonally? In other words, have you suffered because of it?
- Do you spend a fair amount of time and energy using the substance or engaging in the activity?
- Have you tried to quit—only to discover that you have fallen into a pattern of withdrawing and relapsing?

Other critical areas you may wish to assess as you consider whether or not your behavior is addictive include why you do it and when you do it. Does it, for example, enable you to "check out" of life for awhile? Do you tend to do it when you are feeling something that makes you uncomfortable, such as anxiety, insecurity, stress, or anger? And, do you feel like you need it to survive whatever you are facing or feeling? Along with Judith Wright (2003) in her book There Must Be More Than This, I would also encourage you to think about what the substance or activity makes you feel—aside from pleasure, of course. Are you defensive about it or does it cause you to feel any guilt or shame such that you'd prefer that others not know about it or see you do it? Answering "yes" to these questions as well could suggest that your behavior is addictive.

One other characteristic I would associate with addictive behavior concerns the balance of power in an individual's life. I recall attending a lecture on addictions a number of years ago in which the presenter explained that those who suffer from an addiction often feel powerless to control whatever it is they are using the addiction to avoid. Their "conscious choice" to engage in addictive behaviors seems to afford them a false sense of power or control, when, in truth, it is really the addiction that is controlling them. Ironically enough, the recognition that they cannot seem to control their addictive behavior only serves to exacerbate their feelings of powerlessness which can, in turn, fuel their addiction. This power struggle is all part and parcel of the vicious cycle that characterizes addictive behavior.

Understanding the Problem: What Causes An Addiction?

The many theories that have been proposed to explain the genesis of an addiction seem to suggest that no single cause is responsible for all addictive behaviors. Instead, as was the case with depression and anxiety, an interplay of biological and psychological factors appears to be at work. On the biological side of the scale, both brain chemistry and heredity have been implicated. With regard to the former, do you remember those enormously powerful but very tiny chemicals called neurotransmitters that we discussed with regard to depression and anxiety? Well, they are related to addictive behavior as well, primarily because an addiction can stimulate the brain chemicals that are most associated with pleasure. In fact, what makes addictions so intransigent is that the changes in brain chemistry they produce program the individual to crave the source of the addiction even more (Mayo, 2011).

With regard to genetics, extensive studies have shown that the familiar adage "apples don't fall far from the tree" is as true with respect to addictions as it is for any other type of inherited disorder, including anxiety and depression. In short, if there is a family history of certain addictions, such as drug or alcohol abuse, an individual is far, far more likely to develop one than if there is not (Mayo, 2011).

On the psychological side of the scale, a number of additional factors have been linked to the development of specific addictions. One such factor is the individual's environment, and here again, parents play a pivotal role as do peer groups. If the parents are themselves addicts or if they are not around to supervise their children and/or monitor their peer group involvement, substance abuse is more likely to result (Mayo, 2011). But parental involvement can also generate other types of addictions as children and "adult children" use substances or activities to compensate for the love they never really received from their physically or emotionally absent parents. By so doing, they are attempting to escape the feelings of rejection and abandonment that are too painful to feel.

Child abuse is another environmental factor that can result in an addiction as individuals attempt to assuage the decidedly unpleasant feelings that physical, sexual and emotional abuse can cause them to experience. The addictions are their way of coping with the "anxiety, depression and loneliness" (Mayo, 2011) that may have resulted from the abuse. Essentially, they are using the addiction to self-medicate. The same can be said for those individuals who are battling specific medical conditions related to addictions, including depression, PTSD, and even ADHD (Mayo, 2011).

Other major stressors can certainly lead to addictions, lending credence to the fact that these same addictions are *never* caused by a personal weakness or by some type of fault that resides within an individual.

They are *always* a response to an individual's experience (biological and/ or psychological). As such, they represent that individual's attempt to cope with this experience. Any time the needs of an individual are not being met or he or she is experiencing uncomfortable feelings, regardless of the cause, an addiction can become a central part of that person's life. Those with a family history of addiction or those with absentee or abusive parents are more likely to develop addictions as are those with other medical conditions such as depression and anxiety, regardless of whether or not they resulted from abuse. Rather than blame the addict for causing his/her addiction, it is far more accurate to say that he or she has not developed healthy coping mechanisms to address his or life experience.

Solving the Problem: Pathways to Healing Addictions

If I were only permitted to make one statement with respect to healing addictions, it would be this one: *In all likelihood, you cannot do it alone.* The most you probably *can* do alone is admit that you have a problem and analyze its various causes with regard to your particular life experience. To begin this process, I want to remind you that an addiction is a sign of a much larger problem. In the self-analytical phase of your healing journey, it is your job to identify what that problem might be by closely examining what causes *you* to pursue your addiction in any given moment. You can do so—not by going "cold turkey" (which rarely works anyway)—but by taking just a moment to stop yourself before you take that first sip or that first puff or that first bite to ask this question: What do I not want to face or feel right now? I am not telling you to stop what you were just about to do (yet). I am merely asking you to pause and reflect upon it for just a moment. If you were to take an additional moment to write your answer to this question down, that would be even better, but for our purposes right now, a moment's pause will suffice.

If you are really serious about getting to the bottom of your addiction and breaking its power over you, this "pause and reflect" strategy is going to lead you to some very painful places, but out of all this pain, peace and healing *will* eventually emerge. What kind of pain am I talking about? Specifically, your reflections may lead you to see that you are (or that you feel) bored, lonely, unloved or unlovable, rejected, abandoned, ashamed, grief-stricken, guilty, anxious, depressed, stressed, afraid, overwhelmed, or empty—to name just a handful of the responses that might come to mind when you honestly answer the aforementioned question. While it's true that you may need the help of a therapist to fully understand and treat your addiction, your initial "pause and reflect" efforts will go a long way toward helping you win the battle since it is much harder to consciously hurt yourself than it is to do so unconsciously—and an addiction is nothing more than an unconscious act of self-harm—whether it be physical, emotional, or spiritual.

As you begin to examine what fuels your addiction, you may find it helpful to keep in mind that the feelings you identify in the "pause and reflect" stage came from somewhere—oftentimes in the past. They were born when someone hurt you in some way, and, at the time, you may have been too young to access the resources you now have at your disposal as an adult. How, for example, does a young child cope with physical, sexual, verbal, or emotional abuse? By burying the pain, and every time she addicts as an adult, she buries that pain even deeper. A critical turning point for all addicts, then, is the recognition that the past can no longer hurt them (unless they allow it to do so via their addiction). It is at this point that they realize they have resources for expressing and addressing the feelings they buried as children. But the buried feelings underlying an addiction may also arise from an addict's more recent past, of course (e.g., when he experiences a major loss). Here again, healing involves accessing appropriate resources to address whatever it is he may be feeling.

In addition to pointing you toward the pain from your distant or recent past, your "pause and reflect" moments may also reveal your lack of fulfillment in the present moment—hence your attempt to escape it with an addiction. Simply put, you may come to see that something is missing in your life. As Judith Wright (2003) points out, you know that you want more out of life, but you have confused the desires of your heart with what your mind thinks it wants. What do I mean by this statement? I mean that you truly desire to fulfill your inner longings, which, by the way, are the same longings we all share as human beings, but you have created an unhealthy substitute for them in the form of an addiction. What are these inner longings? One of my professors in graduate school expressed them as "something to do, someone to love, and something for which to hope." Another one of my professors put it this way: "making a difference, being a blessing rather than a curse to others, and growing up rather than just growing older." The basic human needs to which I am referring are about our relationships to others and to the world in which we live and they revolve around connecting, contributing and growing. Pretty heavy stuff, yes? And that is precisely why, short of some serious introspection and reflection, so many of us confuse our basic human needs with an addiction that can never, ever satisfy us.

You have heard it before: You cannot buy love and no amount of substances you ingest or material goods you purchase or distractions you employ can satisfy these basic human needs. Until you begin to distinguish your needs from whatever addictive substance or activity you have substituted for them, you will not be able to break free of the addictive cycle in which you find yourself caught and you will not be able to see that your addiction continues to make a promise it cannot ever keep by providing you with a temporary fix but no lasting or meaningful satisfaction or fulfillment. Every time you come down from your "high," whatever it is, absolutely nothing will have changed.

So, as you "pause and reflect," you may also wish to consider which of your basic human needs is not being met. Is there a lack of love and connection in your life? Do you feel as though you are not contributing enough or as though you do not really matter? Do you feel that you are not maturing or that you are not gaining greater wisdom? Which of your deeper human needs remains unsatisfied?

One final point to keep in mind during your "pause and reflect" process is that all addictions are, on some level, a form of resistance. In other words, we addict because there is something in our life we cannot accept … whether it is that a parent didn't really love us or that we don't know how to cope with our loneliness or that we don't know how to handle stress. Rather than accept the feeling or situation and just be with it and breathe our way through it, we opt to escape it with our addictive behavior. It is as though we are afraid that whatever we are attempting to escape is too much for us to bear. Part of healing from an addiction, however, is recognizing that the addiction itself is far more likely to harm us—or even kill us—than whatever it is we are using it to escape. Life by its very nature is difficult and bad things really do happen to good people. Peacefully (and notice I didn't say happily) accepting the nature of human life rather than attempting to resist or escape its most painful realities will go a long way toward aiding us in our addiction recovery work.

Asking For Help

As noted earlier, when it comes to healing an addiction, admitting you have a problem and reflecting upon its causes is only half the battle. The real work begins when you make a conscious choice to do something about it. To this end, your best bet is to reach out for help. In order to do so effectively, you need to make (and keep) three promises to yourself. First and foremost, you need to put your shame in your back pocket and promise yourself that it will remain there while you are healing. The shame your addiction undoubtedly causes you to feel is a very powerful deterrent to healing. Addicts don't want anyone to know that they engage in or cannot control their addictive behaviors. If you can make and keep this first promise to yourself, however, not only will you be able to reach out for help but you will also take great comfort in discovering just how many people do exactly what it is that you have been too ashamed to admit that you do as well—and many of these same people will be enormously helpful to you as you embark on your own healing journey.

Secondly, you must reject what feels like your best friend and/or your best friends and find a new friend and a new community of support. I am speaking metaphorically here, but my meaning is twofold: An addiction can feel like your best friend. It comforts you, it's very reliable, it makes you feel good when you are feeling down, and it's always there for you—day or night. In this regard, it's a hard friend to leave, but leave it you must or it may very well become your worst enemy. The other "friends" you must leave—if you have them—are those who share your addiction. If they are not yet ready to heal, they will only undermine your own attempt to do so.

Finally, you must promise yourself that you will not give up if you relapse—and you may relapse. Addiction recovery can be a two steps forward, three steps backward process, but eventually, with a sincere commitment to heal, you *will* move forward, despite the temptations that assail you. Put simply, when it comes to healing an addiction, you may lose a few battles along the way, but if you keep this last promise to yourself, you will most definitely win the war. It's all about perseverance, and perseverance eventually leads to mastery.

Once you've made (and intend to keep) these three promises to yourself, you will be ready to seek the kinds of assistance that are described below.

> *Medical Treatment:* Certain addictions may be treated with medication—either to wean you off a highly addictive drug like heroine or to address an underlying medical condition, such as depression or anxiety, that may, in part, be responsible for your addiction.

> *Counseling:* Depending upon the nature of the addiction, you may need to receive counseling through a treatment center or via a weekly session with a therapist. The focus of addiction recovery counseling is threefold: to address the causes of your addiction (i.e., what you may not wish to face or feel); to treat any additional

issues, such as depression, that you may have; and to provide you with much healthier coping mechanisms. A variety of techniques are used, ranging from Cognitive Behavioral to group therapy, all of which will help you to develop the skills you need to resist your addiction. In counseling, you will learn how to change your situation if you can, or if not, how to change your attitude toward it so that it does not cause you the kind of distress that leads you to addict. You will be encouraged to create a new vision for your future and of who you are and you will learn what steps to take to make this new vision a reality. All in all, addiction recovery counseling is a very hope-filled process because it so powerfully addresses whatever it is that is not working in your life.

Community Support: A recovering alcoholic, whom we know as Bill Wilson, created the very popular Twelve Step Program pathway to healing wherein addicts come together to support one another's efforts to recover. Twelve Step Programs exist for a variety of addictions, though some of the most popular include Alcoholics Anonymous, Adult Children of Alcoholics (ACOA), Narcotics Anonymous, Overeaters Anonymous, and Gamblers Anonymous. The twelve steps help addicts to admit they are powerless over their addiction, to ask their "higher power" (whatever they conceive that to be) for assistance, and to make amends to those individuals who may have been hurt by their addiction. Twelve Step Programs have withstood the test of time and have proven to be a highly effective tool for helping individuals gain control over their addictions. If you choose to participate in a Twelve Step Program, you will have the opportunity to attend daily or weekly meetings wherein you can hear the stories of others and/or share your own story in a very safe setting. Twelve Step Programs likewise provide you with a variety of resources, including a personal sponsor to support you (day or night) and a safe place to go when the temptation to relapse is at its strongest. By participating in a Twelve Step Program, not only will you learn that you are not alone but you will also learn how others have coped with the very same "triggers" that led you to develop your addiction.

Alternative Support: Some of the same alternative therapies used to treat anxiety and depression, such as yoga, meditation (or prayerful meditation), and acupuncture are also used to treat addictions such as alcoholism (Mayo, 2012). There are a number of reasons these alternative therapies may benefit those in recovery: they can relieve the stress and anxiety that may be underlying the addiction, they help individuals to center themselves in the present moment without feeling overwhelmed by it, they lend themselves to the kind of reflective thinking that can help addicts discover the source of their addiction, they balance or rebalance energy, and they provide individuals with "wait time"— that is, time to make the choice not to addict. These alternative therapies constitute a healthy coping mechanism in the face of whatever it is an individual would like to avoid.

As you reach out for help, you may likewise find it useful to develop creative ways to address your addiction in much the same way you can address depression or anxiety. These creative activities can replace your addictions at the same time they afford you the opportunity to express whatever it is you have buried beneath your addiction. So, as you embark on your healing journey, do not discount the option of turning to music, poetry, literature, prayer (if you are so inclined), nature and/or writing.

One final point I believe it is vitally important for you to remember as you begin your addiction recovery work is the same one I made with regard to depression and anxiety, namely, that *you are not your addiction.* You are not even an "addict." I have only used that term in this chapter for lack of a better one. What you are is a beautiful human being who is temporarily struggling with certain addictive behaviors. If you can identify with your authentic self in this way rather than with your addiction(s), you will find within that same self the power you need to control the behaviors that seem to be controlling you.

Final Remarks

In the end, every addiction is about choice: we choose how to view the painful events in our lives, namely as opportunities for personal growth or as catalysts for our own self-destruction. We choose whether to face these painful events and let them go, recognizing that they can no longer hurt us, or we choose to let them control us by pursuing an addiction. And, finally, we choose whether or not to heal our addiction once it has taken hold of us. The decision to heal may feel overwhelming on a number of different levels, most especially because it involves addressing a feeling or a situation we'd rather not acknowledge and because it can be a time-consuming process, the outcome of which does not seem guaranteed, given our propensity to relapse. However, when faced with the alternative, I'd say that healing an addiction is time very well spent and that there is no better time to do so than during our college years when we are in the process of closely examining who we are and what we want out of life. I would also argue that if we have time to pursue our addictions, then we have time to heal them. Remember: healing an addiction is not just about saying NO. It's about saying YES to a future only you can create for yourself, a future you are in college to achieve, and a future where, despite what you may have been told or have come to believe, your most cherished dreams really *can* come true.

5

When You Hunger For More:

Understanding Eating Disorders

*When I write of hunger, I am really writing about
love and the hunger for it, and warmth and the love
of it ... and it is all one.*

--M.F.K. Fisher

Life itself is the proper binge.

--Julia Child

If you are tempted to skip reading this chapter because you think it's
about *women* who suffer from anorexia or bulimia—think again. While
I do discuss specific eating disorders on the following pages—primarily
because they affect so many college students (male and female)—this
particular chapter is really about the complicated relationship we *all*
have with food. It's about not eating what we should, when we should,
and why we should. At its most basic level, it's also about another type of
addictive behavior that can markedly sabotage your attempts to achieve
success in college and in life.

Defining the Problem: What Is An Eating Disorder?

To encompass all of the points made below, I think it best to define an eating disorder very broadly as a "dysfunctional (or problematic) relationship with the food we eat." This problematic relationship can be either mild or severe. A mild eating disorder is sometimes called "emotional eating"—that is, the kind of eating we do when we are "stuffing" certain feelings or states of being such as loneliness, boredom, depression, anxiety, and stress. In other words, we are eating to distract ourselves from unpleasant sensations—not because we are physically hungry. In the case of emotional eating, we are, in fact, hungry—but not for food. We're hungry for something else, such as deeper connections or physical relief, but we are using food as a substitute for these unacknowledged needs. As you can see if you have finished reading Chapter 4, some of the same factors that inform other addictive behaviors can lead to emotional eating as well. For example, our lack of love, our need for power/control, our desire for instant rewards, and our attempt to comfort or anesthetize ourselves can all result in a mild eating disorder.

The primary differences between mild and severe eating disorders (such as anorexia and bulimia) are the time we spend on them, the single-minded focus on food and weight they perpetuate, our inability to control them, and the physical harm they do to us. Emotional eating can become habitual, but we are not always powerless to stop it and it is not usually associated with other more serious medical conditions. In contrast, severe eating disorders are not usually behaviors we can discontinue on our own and they can result in serious physical harm. As is the case with every personal barrier to college success discussed in this book, we are always talking about a continuum of behavior from mild to severe, regardless of the barrier itself. And, like every other barrier to success, if left untreated, eating disorders will always thwart our efforts to reach our potential because they, too, consume our attention, our energy, and our resources. They likewise prevent us from addressing the real culprit—namely, that which has caused us to develop a dysfunctional relationship with food in the first place. Only when we free ourselves from whatever that is will we truly be able to pursue the goals we came to college to achieve. Put in the form of a question, how can anyone successfully pursue a goal if she is overly focused on food and/or weight while simultaneously avoiding underlying issues that prevent her from reaching her unique potential?

Identifying the Problem: How Do I Know If I Have An Eating Disorder?

Since just about everyone has a complicated relationship with food, it is highly likely that, on some level, you, too, are affected by your eating habits—especially if the stress of college life is taking its toll on you. The question to consider is: How serious are the effects of your behaviors with respect to your attempts to achieve your goals? Remember: anything that distracts or physically harms you constitutes a potentially significant barrier to your success.

To this end, as you consider whether or not your relationship with food is problematic, you may find it helpful to learn to recognize the symptoms of both mild and severe eating disorders. With regard to the former, lest you think that a mild eating disorder is an essentially harmless habit, please remember that mild eating disorders (and/or the dieting they engender) very often lead to more severe ones (Mayo, 2012). Recognizing your vulnerability with respect to food will go a long way toward helping you overcome this particular barrier to college success.

So, how do you know if you have a mild eating disorder? I recommend thoughtfully examining when, what, and why you eat. The following questions will guide your explorations in this area:

- Do you tend to eat only when you are experiencing the symptoms of physical hunger or do you eat when you are upset bored, or stressed? Do you ever use food to reward yourself for something?

- Do you have designated meal times or do you eat erratically (often in response to something external)?
- Do you keep eating even after you feel full? Do you sometimes (or often) feel stuffed after eating (apart from Thanksgiving Day)?
- Do you primarily eat healthy foods that nourish your body or do you frequently consume foods that are high in sugar, fat, and salt?
- Do you prefer eating alone and do you tend to eat more when you are by yourself than when you are with others?
- Do you ever feel ashamed about what or how much you eat?
- Do you tend to "zone out" while eating such that you might not realize or remember what or how much you just ate?
- Do you ever feel out of control when you eat or do you feel like you control what you eat more than you should?
- Do you tend to eat quickly?
- Do you find yourself thinking about food a lot— when you'll eat again, what you'll eat, how much you'll eat, and so forth?
- Do you diet or exercise or use OTC medications in response to your eating habits?

If your answers to these questions were primarily affirmative and if they indicate that you tend to eat unhealthy foods erratically in response to physical or emotional stress, there is a good chance you have or are at risk for developing a mild eating disorder since such responses and tendencies suggest that your eating habits are somewhat similar to those that are seen in individuals with anorexia or bulimia. Affirmative responses also suggest that you are using food as a drug rather than as a source of nourishment or sustenance.

Severe eating disorders are much easier to identify than are mild ones and do not require a high degree of self-examination in this regard. They are characterized by specific behaviors over which an individual has no control. If you suffer from anorexia nervosa, you are terrified of gaining weight, no matter how thin you are, and you will do whatever it takes, including under eating and over exercising, to avoid weight gain. You may believe you are overweight even if you are skeletally thin, and a disproportionate degree of your self-worth is related to how much you weigh (Mayo, 2012). The popular PBS video, Dying to Be Thin, is very aptly titled since anorexia can—and does—kill those who are afflicted with it. It is, by every definition, a slow form of self-starvation.

Identifiable symptoms of anorexia include weight loss, low energy, feeling dizzy or passing out, hair thinning or loss, the growth of soft fuzzy hair on the body, the cessation of periods (in women), the loss of testosterone (in men), insomnia, electrolyte imbalances, gastrointestinal problems, heart palpitations, anemia, dehydration, premature bone loss, and swelling (Mayo, 2012). All of these symptoms result from self-starvation, the effects of which may not be "fully reversible" (Mayo, 2012).

Specific behaviors associated with anorexia nervosa include refusal to eat (even when hungry), over exercising, eating only foods very low in calories, eating very small bites of food, frequently weighing oneself, lying about food intake, socially withdrawing, being preoccupied with food, losing interest in sex, and viewing oneself as "fat" even when moderately or severely underweight (Mayo, 2012). Finally, many anorexics also suffer from other mental health concerns, such as depression, anxiety (including OCD), personality disorders, and substance abuse (Mayo, 2012).

A close cousin of anorexia nervosa is bulimia nervosa. If you have it, you are also overly focused on how much you weigh but rather than starve yourself, you eat an excessive amount of food and then eliminate it by vomiting, exercising, or using "laxatives, diuretics, or enemas" (Mayo, 2012). You may also misuse "dietary supplements or herbal products for weight loss" (Mayo, 2012). Unlike anorexics, "people with bulimia can fall within the normal range for their age and weight … but like people with anorexia, they often fear gaining weight, want desperately to lose weight, and are intensely unhappy with their body size and shape" (NIMH, 2011).

Specific symptoms of bulimia nervosa include throat pain or inflammation, neck or gland swelling, tooth decay, gastrointestinal distress, dehydration, and electrolyte problems (NIMH, 2011).

Specific behaviors associated with bulimia nervosa include a preoccupation with "body shape and weight," severe overeating, excessively exercising, feeling badly about one's body, and retreating to the restroom during or immediately following a meal (Mayo, 2012). The binge purge cycle that characterizes bulimia nervosa is always performed in private and may generate a tremendous amount of shame. Additionally, as was the case with anorexia nervosa, those with bulimia nervosa often suffer from accompanying issues such as depression and anxiety—inclusive of OCD—as well as a low regard for self, a tendency toward perfectionism and/or impulsivity, and unresolved anger (Mayo, 2012).

And, finally, there is the most common eating disorder, also known as "binge eating disorder" or "compulsive eating." If you suffer from binge eating disorder, you consume very large amounts of food on a regular basis. Binge eaters may or may not be overweight, depending upon how often their binges occur, but they do engage in specific food-related behaviors, including consuming foods despite feeling full, eating food very quickly, sensing they are not in control of their eating, constantly dieting, often eating alone, and almost always feeling badly about their eating habits (Mayo, 2012). Binge eaters frequently feel ashamed of their eating behaviors and, like those with anorexia nervosa or bulimia nervosa, they, too, suffer from depression, anxiety, or substance abuse (Mayo, 2012).

Given the extent of the physical and psychological effects of eating disorders, it should be clear by now why they do indeed significantly affect a college student's ability to reach his or her potential. The time they consume, the shame they produce, and the toll they take on body, mind and spirit all but destroy an individual's chances of fully realizing the dreams he or she first entered college to pursue. So, what, exactly would cause someone to sacrifice so much for his or her eating disorder? As the following section illustrates, the answer to this question is a complex one.

Understanding the Problem: What Causes Eating Disorders?

There are many potential causes of eating disorders, some of which are biological and some of which are environmental. At this point in our discussion, it should come as no surprise that those pesky little neurotransmitters we discussed with respect to depression, anxiety, and addictions are likewise thought to influence the development of eating disorders such as anorexia nervosa (Mayo, 2012), perhaps because they are responsible for both appetite and feelings of pleasure. As noted above, food can be used as a drug, and using it in this way could potentially result in an eating disorder. Researchers have also theorized that "genes ... make certain people more vulnerable to developing eating disorders" and that "people with first-degree relatives—siblings or parents—with an eating disorder may be more likely to develop [one] too" (Mayo, 2012).

Environmentally speaking, causes of eating disorders are in no short supply. Given that food is a socially acceptable and readily available drug, it stands to reason that some of the same factors that influence the development of drug addictions, such as a poor self-regard, anger management issues, traumatic experiences, depression, anxiety, and major life transitions may also trigger the development of an eating disorder (Mayo, 2012). In the case of food, however, the purpose of its use as a drug is twofold, depending upon the nature of the disorder. On the one hand, food can be used to soothe, to distract, or to escape and, on the other, it can be used to attain perfection for those who have been made to feel "less than" in general or "less than perfect" in particular. In this sense, food becomes a vehicle for achieving the perfection an individual feels is lacking in himself once he creates the perfect body with the perfect weight.

Those who feel "less than" in response to specific experiences such as child abuse and those who feel they can't control their life circumstances may also turn to food regulation to gain a sense of power. Though they may not be able to control what is happening in their abusive families, for example, they can control when, what, and how much they eat. They can also use food to control their relationships or their proximity to other people. For example, if someone has been sexually abused, she can use food to make herself disappear (to avoid being noticed) or to insulate herself (to avoid being touched and to feel safe). What those who use food as a source of control do not realize, however, is that, like all addictive or compulsive behaviors, their eating disorder is controlling them and not the other way around.

In addition to unpredictable and often uncontrollable environmental factors, our society's concept of beauty may likewise influence the development of eating disorders. "Thin is in," and it always has been so much so that "success and worth are often equated with being thin" (Mayo, 2012). The beauty myth is all around us—on every magazine cover, in every commercial, on every billboard, and in every Hollywood movie. Such images are enormously powerful determinants of human behavior if we are exposed to them often enough and if we are already at risk for developing an eating disorder.

Speaking of risk factors, it should be noted at this point that there are a number of them that have been linked to the development of an eating disorder. Specifically, eating disorders are more common in women than in men (with the exception of binge eating disorder) and they are more likely to surface during one's teenage or college years than at any other time (Mayo, 2012). Dieting is also a noted catalyst for eating disorders as are major life transitions such as "changing schools, moving, landing a new job, or a relationship break up" (Mayo, 2012). In all of these cases, food—and its regulation—is once again used to "stuff" painful emotions and/or achieve a sense of control in the face of unsettling or unwelcome changes. Another contributing factor to eating disorders relates to an individual's chosen vocation or avocation. People who are involved in certain athletic or artistic endeavors (such as ballet, gymnastics, acting, running and wrestling) are likewise at greater risk for developing problematic relationships with food (Mayo, 2012).

One other potential cause of eating disorders is not one that you will probably find in any scientific or medical literature on the subject. Based on my own observations, however, I have always thought that some eating disorders may, in fact, result from the absence of love in an individual's life. Love, like food, is a basic human need, and it is fairly easy to use one to compensate for the lack of the other. When we overeat, we may be attempting, albeit unsuccessfully, to fill an as yet unfulfilled need for loving relationships in our lives, and when we under eat, we may be treating our bodies the way we feel about ourselves (i.e., unlovable).

In the end, there is no single cause of eating disorders. What results in a problematic relationship with food no doubt arises from a combination of factors, some biological and some environmental, that are specific to the individual who develops the disorder. Understanding what may be causing your eating disorder, be it mild or severe, however, will help you learn to manage it so that it stops hurting you. This vital self knowledge is part and parcel of the healing process and is discussed at length in the following section.

Solving the Problem: Pathways to Healing Eating Disorders

As is the case with all addictive-like behaviors, eating disorders included, there is no definitive cure for them (Mayo, 2012), but there are ways to manage them so that you can focus on what is truly important to you, namely, achieving whatever goals you have set for yourself. As you work to gain control over your eating disorder, you will also enjoy a much higher quality of life.

Asking for Help

As always, your first step toward mastery is to admit that you have a problem with food. Once you do so, you will be ready to seek assistance from a variety of resources—and you probably *will* need to seek their assistance—especially given the many physical and psychological issues associated with eating disorders. To this end, you will find below a number of resources from which you will derive great benefit once you decide that you are ready to begin this possibly life-long (and potentially life-saving) journey.

> *Your Primary Doctor:* Because eating disorders can lead to a variety of physical symptoms, ranging from digestive problems to irregular heartbeats, you may need to seek the assistance of a medical doctor. If you've suffered an electrolyte imbalance or esophageal damage, for example, you obviously cannot treat these conditions on your own. In extreme cases, you may need to be temporarily hospitalized to address the medical issues your eating disorder has caused, but hospitalization is more the exception than the norm. Finally, in addition to treating medical conditions resulting from your eating disorder, your doctor can also prescribe certain vitamins and minerals as well as medications, such as antidepressants, anti-psychotics, or mood stabilizers that may help to address underlying causes of your eating disorder and/or to control binging and purging (NIMH, 2011).

> *Dieticians:* At its most fundamental level, an eating disorder is about balance—or the lack of it. If you have an eating disorder, you are definitely not adhering to a balanced diet. In all likelihood, you are either consuming far too many sugar, salt, fat or carb-filled foods or you are depriving your body of the valuable nutrients it needs to survive and to perform at an optimal level. Because you have lost sight of what constitutes a balanced diet and because you may likewise need to gain an understanding of necessary (and normal) caloric intakes to assuage your fear of weight gain, meeting with a registered

dietician to develop an appropriate nutritional plan for you may be an essential part of your healing process (Mayo, 2012). A dietician can teach you what to eat, when to eat, and how to eat ... all behaviors that you need to re-learn to achieve the nutritional balance your eating disorder has disturbed or destroyed.

Individual Counseling: If you review the causes of eating disorders discussed earlier in this chapter, you will better apprehend why counseling therapy is such a necessary step on your healing journey. When it comes to eating disorders, you will benefit from therapy on two levels: First, you will address whatever may be causing you to over or under eat. If, for example, you have unresolved grief or if you are unable to handle stress or if you suffer from depression or anxiety, you can use your counseling sessions to explore these issues and to create more appropriate coping mechanisms ... just as you would for an addiction. In truth, you neither wish to starve yourself nor do you wish to eat yourself into oblivion. You are, in part, reacting to something significant that has upset you. Counseling will help you learn how to cope with whatever has caused your distress. In some cases, you may need to invite your family members to join you for some counseling sessions if it is determined that issues with your family relate to your eating disorder (Mayo, 2012). The other manner in which counseling can help you concerns how you think about food, weight, body image, and the media's messages about each of them. Earlier in our discussion of personal barriers to college success, we talked about "thinking yourself sick and well" with regard to depression and anxiety, and the same pattern is true with respect to food. How you think about food, weight, your body, and yourself can most assuredly perpetuate an eating disorder. Counseling can help you develop a more balanced way of thinking about each of these critical areas.

Group Counseling: By their very nature, eating disorders are quite isolating. No one wants to be caught (or criticized for) binging, purging or abstaining from food. Those who suffer from eating disorders, even mild ones, often feel a great deal of shame or guilt with regard to their eating behaviors, and few feelings promote social isolation as readily as these two do. Group therapy can help people with eating disorders overcome this isolation and it can ease feelings of guilt and shame once these individuals realize they are most definitely not alone. Group therapy can also provide participants with a number of helpful resources that they may not have known were available. There are a variety of groups to choose from, ranging from the Twelve Step Program "Overeaters Anonymous" to those run by licensed professionals. Combining individual counseling with group therapy may be especially beneficial to those with severe eating disorders.

Learning to Help Yourself

At the same time you are seeking professional assistance to address your problematic relationship with food, you can also employ a number of self-help strategies to enhance and maintain your healing efforts. Because eating disorders may result from or relate to depression, anxiety, grief, addictions, stress, and low self-esteem, all personal barriers to college success discussed in this book, you may wish to review the self-help techniques presented in previous or successive chapters in addition to those you will find below. As you read what follows, you will soon discover that many of these strategies necessitate changing both your thoughts and your behaviors—a reality that will, in all probability, initially cause you some discomfort. Such is the nature of change, however. It will always make you feel uncomfortable at first, but eventually, your new thoughts and behaviors will become old habits—in this case, old, much healthier eating habits.

Change or Break the Rules: If you have an eating disorder, you play by certain rules. Depending upon the nature of your condition, these rules may cause you to portion your food, to constantly weigh yourself, to eat until you're stuffed, to eat while distracted or on the run, to eat whatever you want whenever you want, or to not eat at all for long periods of time. Healing from an eating disorder means replacing these rigid, overindulgent, self-destructive rules with ones that are both balanced and healthy. You will find such rules in just about every book or article that has ever been written on the topic of eating disorders, but for now, I will offer you a brief summary of some of the most frequently recommended ones:

- DO eat healthy foods when you are hungry and DO stop eating as soon as you feel full
- DO eat at the same times each day and DO include light snacks between meals
- DO NOT skip meals
- DO NOT diet—and you won't need to if you eat healthfully
- DO NOT eat while engaged in any other type of activity
- DO NOT eat when you are upset.

Not only will your new rules help you to manage your eating disorder but they will also help you to regulate your metabolism which, in turn, will help you to regulate your weight. In truth, diets actually have the opposite effect.

Mistrust Your Judgment: I normally tell students to trust their judgment but not in the case of eating disorders. As hard as it may be for you to admit this fact to yourself, if you have an eating disorder, it is highly likely that you suffer from a distorted body and/or self image, both of which can cause you to starve or to stuff yourself. As you heal, remember that you are not the best judge of your character or appearance at the moment and resist the urge to look in the mirror, to second guess your new eating habits, or to constantly weigh yourself (Mayo, 2012).

Read: In the case of eating disorders, knowledge really is power. Make a commitment to learn about the various types of eating disorders, from mild to severe, and to practice the strategies suggested by the authors of these books until you find the right combination for you.

Silence Your Inner Critic: You will learn about this strategy in counseling, but you can also practice it on your own. We all have an inner critic, that negative voice that tells us we aren't good enough, smart enough, talented enough or thin enough. Believe it or not, the messages your inner critic sends you may, in part, be causing you to over or under eat. Doing so is your way of silencing this critic, but you know from experience that it doesn't work. The voice just gets louder and, as a result, the problematic behavior it engenders merely intensifies. The only way to silence this critic is to replace its messages with those of your inner champion … that kind, gentle, loving voice that is housed deep within your heart and generates messages such as: "I am both loved and lovable. I am deserving of respect. I am smart and beautiful (or handsome) and talented and perfect just as I am. Nothing anyone says or does to me can diminish me in any way." Consistently practicing these self-affirming thoughts will help to counter the self-destructive ones that serve to feed your eating disorder.

Silence the Media: If you need to take a break from your radio, television, computer, or favorite magazines to create a more balanced view of what it means to be a successful and beautiful human being, then do it. As humans, we *do* respond to what we allow ourselves to see, to hear, and to read. If you have the need to abstain from certain foods or to purge yourself of whatever you just ate, try instead to abstain from media images and to purge your psyche of all the lies they tell you about how you should look and who you should be. I am not suggesting that you permanently discard the media from your life, of course. I am merely encouraging you to take a break from its all too pervasive influence until you can create a more balanced perspective of beauty and success.

Connect and Disconnect: With regard to connection, not only is an eating disorder more likely to be thwarted in the presence of others (due to the shame factor) but the supportive presence of others may also distract you from your pain or help you heal as you begin to share this pain with those you trust. As is the case with every personal barrier to college success discussed in this book, those who really care about you will want to help you, so don't be afraid to ask for their help in this way. With respect to disconnecting, if you find yourself surrounded by friends who are overly focused on food, weight, dieting, and body image, then it may be time to branch out and expand your connections to include more positive role models—that is, people who are focused on other types of beauty, such as inner beauty and natural beauty. Again, it's all about monitoring what you take into your mind (i.e., what you see and what you hear).

Pause and Reflect: The same strategy I suggested in Chapter 4 for other addictive behaviors applies to eating disorders as well. This strategy, which is most applicable to overeating, is designed to help you identify what may be causing you to stuff your feelings with food. The next time you are tempted to binge, pause for just a moment and ask yourself: "What don't I want to face or feel right now?" As you learn to identify the cause of your behavior, you can take appropriate steps to address it. Until you identify what is making you overeat, it is highly unlikely that this behavior will resolve on its own.

Create Healthy Distractions: After you begin to identify what is causing you to overeat or to be overly focused on food/weight in general, you can create healthy ways to distract yourself from these unhealthy behaviors. These healthy distractions might, for example, include painting, drawing, singing, dancing, gardening, writing, sculpting, acting, sailing, reading, volunteering, practicing the martial arts, or meditating. The goal is to find something you enjoy, something that calms you, and something that completely captures your attention so that the anxieties that may be fueling your eating disorder are gradually disarmed. As noted in Chapter 2, if you use healthy distractions to shift the focus of your attention to something beyond your anxieties, you will lessen their power over you. An added benefit of these healthy distractions is that they often lead to the discovery of hidden talents that can make you feel better about yourself, a reality that very definitely counters the need to over or under eat.

Watch How You Move: I usually encourage students to exercise in response to many of the personal barriers to college success discussed in this book (since it can do wonders for depression, anxiety, grief, and stress), but in the case of eating disorders, I would suggest that you proceed with caution primarily because compulsive exercise is one of the ways individuals with these conditions "manage" their diet (Mayo, 2012). In addition, you may not have the health needed to sustain an exercise program if you have not been eating well. Thus, I would encourage you to consult with your doctor as you determine how much exercise is appropriate for you during the various stages of healing. If exercise has been a part of your routine, I would also encourage you to explore gentle movements such as yoga and Tai Chi, primarily because they can help you address additional issues, such as depression, anxiety, and stress that may, in part, be contributing to your eating habits.

Final Remarks

Everyone who suffers from problem eating, whether mild or severe, is faced with a choice: to be or not to be. I am not talking about choosing to live or to die in the literal sense, though, in the severest cases, I could. I am, instead, referring to the quality of life we choose to lead. An eating disorder significantly diminishes that quality by robbing us of our time, our energy, our health, our self-regard, and, perhaps most importantly, our ability to realize our full potential and to revel in our successes. As is the case with all addictive behaviors, an eating disorder is both a pervasive and persistent thief, but like all thieves, it can be caught and ultimately controlled. The choice is yours to make; its consequences are not. Only you can decide to be or not to be ... fully alive, fully nourished, fully satisfied, and fully free.

6

When You're Running On Empty:

Understanding Stress

Rule Number 1 is, don't sweat the small stuff. Rule Number 2 is, it's all small stuff. And if you can't fight, and you can't flee, flow.
--Robert S. Eliot

Every stress leaves an indelible scar, and the organism pays for its survival after a stressful situation by becoming a little older.
--Hans Salye

Have you noticed how many times the word "stress" appears in this book? If not, and if you were to review the foregoing and successive chapters, you would find that "stress" is mentioned in every one of them—often more than once. Why is that? Because stress either causes or results from every personal barrier to college success discussed in this book. It is also the most unavoidable and, inarguably, the most powerful barrier to success you will encounter as a college student. Indeed, no one is immune to stress—which may well explain why not a day goes by without at least one of my students describing him or herself as "totally stressed out." In this chapter, you will learn to recognize and manage your own stressors before you begin to experience their very destructive effects ... and I do not use the word "destructive" lightly. At best, unchecked stress prevents you from achieving your goals, and, at worst, it can kill you. Thus, it is definitely worth learning to recognize and manage your particular stressors before they significantly hinder (or sabotage altogether) even your most valiant attempts to achieve success.

Defining the Problem: What Is Stress?

Simply put, stress is a physical and/or psychological response to a "perceived threat" (Mayo, 2011) that can itself be either physical or psychological. These threats range from being chased down a dark alley by a masked gunman to the discomfort we experience in the face of a major transition that upsets our sense of stability or security (e.g., moving, starting a new job, losing a loved one, graduating, getting married, and so forth). Notice that even positive events, such as weddings and graduations, can cause stress.

The type of stress we experience is either acute or chronic (Mayo, 2010). Acute stress might also be called "new stress" or "immediate stress" because it results from specific incidents we experience, such as losing a job or failing the course we needed to graduate. Acute stress lasts only as long as it takes to recover from whatever has happened (or is happening) to us. Chronic stress "occurs when acute stressors pile up and stick around" (Mayo, 2010) and would include, for example, living in an abusive environment or being forced to attend a college or university that we dislike. The cause of the stress that results from these chronic situations is twofold: the hardship itself—whatever that is (physical, emotional or financial)—as well as our inability to do anything about it.

While both types of stress can be dangerous, depending upon how they affect the individual, chronic stress is more likely to cause the kinds of health problems discussed in the following section (Mayo, 2010). However, it is also possible for an individual to remain chronically stressed if he or she strongly reacts to every upset and/or constantly engages in catastrophic thinking about future events—real or imagined. Are you beginning to see a pattern? We are once again talking about "thinking ourselves sick," and when we tend to generate self-distressing thoughts rather than self de-stressing ones, the higher our stress levels will be— regardless of the stressor itself.

Identifying the Problem: How Do I Know If I Am Stressed?

Even though a number of my students describe themselves as stressed, not all of them are able to recognize the specific symptoms of stress, nor are they privy to the destructive effects these same symptoms can have on their lives. Additionally, a number of them have not made the connection between stress and other personal barriers to college success, including depression, anxiety, and addictive behaviors.

To truly recognize the presence of stress in your life, you need to closely examine three areas: how you feel physically, how you feel emotionally, and how you behave. Why? Because stress affects thoughts, feelings and behaviors (Mayo, 2011). As noted above, we are talking about a physical and a psychological phenomenon. With regard to the latter, stress has both an immediate and a potentially long-term set of effects on the body. The body's immediate reaction to a stressor is one with which you are probably already familiar and is known as the "fight or flight response." Put simply, any potential threat to a person's safety or well-being sets off a chain reaction in the body that includes the release of powerful hormones, such as adrenaline and cortisol, the purpose of which includes increasing both heart rate and blood pressure, suppressing the appetite, and maximizing the use of glucose for energy (Mayo, 2010)   all so that the body has the capacity either to physically ward off the threat or to escape from it altogether. The fight or flight response is not at all problematic if it is only activated in the face of genuine danger (e.g., the need to save oneself from being hit by an oncoming car). However, the body does not know how to distinguish between genuine danger and all the other stressors that can likewise trigger its fight or flight response if an individual perceives such stressors as potential threats.

It is at this point that stress becomes dangerous, primarily because the fight or flight response was never meant to be continually activated. When this happens, all sorts of other physical symptoms can appear in the body—some of which are quite harmful. Other physical symptoms that result from stress can include "headaches, muscle tension or pain, chest pain, fatigue, a change in sexual drive, stomach upset, and sleep problems" (Mayo, 2011). Left untreated, these physical manifestations of stress can lead to even more serious health concerns, such as heart disease and depression (Mayo, 2011). In fact, as my own doctors have so often stated, it would not be an exaggeration to state that stress plays a role in many of the illnesses we acquire. Think about it: when do you tend to catch a cold or contract the flu? Most often, it is when you are under high stress or when you have just endured a period of high stress such that your immune system has been compromised.

Behaviorally speaking, stress can cause people to engage in self-destructive or generally unhealthy activities such as smoking or alcohol or drug use (Mayo, 2011) and it is not uncommon for stress to provoke crying over even the most insignificant of incidents, nor is it unusual for stress to occasion bouts of negative and/or catastrophic thinking (Mayo, 2010).

Given the effects of stress on your body, on your mind, and on your behavior, are you beginning to see why it acts as such a significant impediment to your success in college? As noted earlier, if it negatively affects how you feel physically, how you feel emotionally, how you behave, and how you think, effectively addressing your stress may well be the single most powerful determinant of your ability to achieve the goals you have set for yourself as a college student—and that is why it is so vitally important for you to learn how to manage or control your stressors before they begin to manage or control *you*.

Understanding the Problem: What Causes Stress?

Physiologically speaking, you do. If you review the definition of stress that appears at the outset of this chapter, you will note that stress results from your response to a *perceived* threat. But who is doing the perceiving? Again, you are. Thus, the threat that causes you to experience stress may well be specific to you and to your personality. A classic example of this phenomenon can be observed on an airplane flight. Some people experience stress prior to boarding a plane while others choose to take flying lessons and spend every spare moment in the air. Such individuals find this experience exhilarating while many others find it unsettling or even terrifying. Just as it is true that "one man's trash is another man's treasure," so, too, is it true that one person's stressor may be another person's source of excitement or joy.

Another way to conceive of stress as specific to the individual is to recall Shakespeare's words in his famous play <u>Hamlet</u>: "… there is nothing either good or bad but thinking makes it so." When it comes to stress, our thoughts about the trigger can be every bit as powerful as the trigger itself. If we think the trigger is to be feared or if we think we can't control it or that it is going to harm or even destroy us, the more likely we are to experience stress.

As I have observed firsthand, our personalities and temperaments may likewise govern our response to triggers and to the stress they do or do not induce. The classic Type A personality who worries and tends toward perfectionism is more likely to experience a greater range of stress and its negative effects than is the classic Type B personality who tends to "go with the flow." These two personalities view life quite differently and that may well explain why they do not always respond to the stressors they encounter in the same way. Their differing responses in part lend credence to the critical role one's thought process plays in the development of stress. Again, how you think determines how you respond and, as noted above, stress is nothing more than a physical and/or psychological response to something you perceive as threatening.

A past history of chronic stress, such as that which results from growing up in an abusive family or serving in the military during wartime, may likewise cause certain individuals to experience more stress later in life—particularly in the form of post-traumatic stress (Mayo, 2010). I have likewise observed that stress seems to have a cumulative effect on some people—the more of it they experience, the more likely they are to find it lurking around every corner of change in their lives and the less likely they are to deal with it effectively. Like too much of anything else in life, it can wear an individual down relatively quickly.

Given the individual nature of the causal factors associated with stress, are there certain triggers that tend to distress most individuals, regardless of personality type? Of course ... but the level of stress these triggers cause is, again, specific to the individual based on his or her thought process, personality, and life experience. Common stressors for most people might include, for example, work or school performance, money management, public speaking, major transitions or losses, and health or legal issues. For college students, we might add: midterms, finals, oral presentations (or just participating in class), adjusting to campus life, balancing work, school, and family responsibilities, and forging new relationships with peers and professors—to name but a few.

Understanding what may be causing you to experience stress, acute or chronic, will benefit you in two significant ways: First, it will help you avoid or discontinue the unhealthy behaviors that often result from high stress, and second, it will help you choose which of the coping strategies described in the following section will be most beneficial for you.

Solving the Problem: Pathways to Healing Stress

Most of the coping strategies designed to help individuals manage their stress are ones you may adopt and practice on your own and do not necessarily require the assistance of a medical or mental health professional —except where noted below.

Asking for Help

If you suffer from chronic stress or if you believe your stress, acute or chronic, is causing anxiety, depression, addictive behaviors (including eating disorders), or low self-esteem, you should definitely seek the assistance of the professional resources referenced in the foregoing and successive chapters of this book. Most notably, you may benefit from **individual or group counseling** where you will not only receive the support and guidance you need to cope with your particular stressors but you will also address their most serious effects (which do not usually disappear on their own and often require some form of therapeutic intervention). In addition, if your physical health has clearly begun to suffer as a result of chronic or acute stress, you may need to consult a **physician** as well. If your stress is acute and therefore has resulted from a major loss or transition, you may likewise find it very beneficial to seek professional assistance as a kind of preventative measure. Remember: stress can have a cumulative effect, so the sooner you learn how to cope with whatever is causing you to experience it, the better. What you learn about stress management via professional assistance will not only help you manage your current stressor but it will also help you more effectively handle whatever stressors you encounter in the future. Finally, if you do choose to seek professional assistance to manage your stress, you may likewise benefit from a number of **alternative treatments**, including **acupuncture, yoga, Tai Chi, biofeedback, and massage therapy.**

Learning to Help Yourself

Regardless of whether or not you choose to seek professional assistance as a stress management tool, you will nonetheless derive great benefit from a variety of proven self-help strategies for stress, each of which is described below.

Watch What You Eat: When we are under stress, we not only tend to over or under eat but we also tend to consume too many unhealthy foods when we do eat (i.e., those especially high in sugar, fat, and salt). These substances can actually serve to aggravate the physical and emotional symptoms of stress that we may be experiencing (e.g., high blood pressure). Yes, eating a carton of ice cream in response to stress may feel good at the moment, but monitor how you feel physically and emotionally thereafter and how these feelings and sensations serve to exacerbate rather than ameliorate your stress levels, especially if you begin to gain weight as a result of your stress-induced eating habits. Eating well will go a long way toward helping you manage stress by providing your body and your mind with the valuable nutrients they need to ward off the negative effects of stress.

Try Vigorous Exercise: Since I have mentioned exercise in each of the foregoing chapters, by now you should be quite familiar with how it benefits both your body and your mind, but when it comes to stress, exercise has also been linked to a "stress buffering effect" in the "brain circuit known to be involved in emotional regulation" (NIMH, 2011). Put another way, exercise does, in fact, reduce your stress levels at the same time it helps to combat the effects of stress on the body, ranging from irregular heartbeats to depression. When it comes to stress management, I recommend an hour of exercise per day, although as little as twenty minutes is still beneficial. In truth, the commitment to a daily program of exercise is probably more important than the actual minutes clocked. Finally, like eating well, exercise will also help you feel better about yourself, and the better you feel about yourself, the more in control of your stress you will be.

Try Gentle Exercise: In this category of exercise, I would include practices I mention above such as Tai Chi, yoga, and certain martial arts activities. These types of exercise reduce stress in a different way via gentle movements and deep breathing. Yoga in particular has been shown to reduce stress (Mayo, 2013) and Tai Chi decreases its negative effects along with those resulting from "a variety of other health conditions" (Mayo, 2012).

Meditate: It does not matter how you choose to meditate. The very act of quieting yourself, breathing slowly and deeply, progressively relaxing your muscles, and repeating a calming phrase such as "I am at peace" or visualizing a tranquil scene can very effectively counter stress and its negative effects, most notably anxiety, binge eating, depression, cancer, high blood pressure, substance abuse, and insomnia (Mayo, 2011). One of my favorite meditations is to mentally place myself on a secluded beach, list my triggers on a piece of paper or on the sand and then imagine myself throwing the paper list into a huge bonfire or watching the waves gently erase the ones I've sketched in the sand. If you are so inclined, you may also wish to engage in prayerful meditation. There is something about handing over one's triggers to a "higher power" that can be very calming. The same holds true with regard to the Serenity Prayer where one asks for the peace to accept what one cannot change, the courage to change what one can, and the wisdom to know the difference. When it comes to meditation or prayerful meditation, there is no right, wrong or "one size fits all" way to do it. You will need to find what works for you. Trying to copy someone else's techniques in this area may only serve to increase your stress rather than to alleviate it.

Listen to Thoreau and to D.A.R.E.: The eminent American author, Henry David Thoreau, enjoins us to "Simplify, simplify," and the anti-drug campaign reminds us to "Just say no." Both messages are very applicable to stress management. We can cause our own stress by surrounding ourselves with clutter and by leading very disorganized, chaotic, or overcommitted lives. If you are stressed, you may need to simplify your life on a number of different levels by eliminating relationships, activities, material objects, and/or commitments that enhance rather than reduce your stress levels. When it comes to excessive commitments, please remember the popular adage that "the word NO is a complete sentence." In other words, you do not have to justify your behavior to anyone. If you need to say "No" to reduce your stress level, then simply say it. The price you pay for continuing to live an overextended life is far greater than any temporary discomfort you may experience if you think you've let someone down. Rest assured that whoever it is will survive, but you may not if you don't slow down and take care of yourself.

Take Some Time Out for Yourself Each Day: This particular stress management technique is part of what it means to take care of yourself—along with exercising and eating well. No one, not even the most revered of saints, can give of him or herself 24/7. No matter how hard you try, eventually your well of energy is going to dry up. Taking time out for yourself each day is one way to ensure that you forever stop running on empty. Specifically, this act of self care and self preservation means doing something you enjoy every day—even if it is only for five to ten minutes. Such activities can include reading, listening to or playing music, gardening, journaling (a personal favorite of mine since it allows for the release of thoughts and feelings that promote stress), taking a hot bath, and so forth. The idea is to choose a pleasurable activity that promotes relaxation. Taking time for yourself will not only help your stress levels but it will also help reduce any feelings of resentment you may have toward your stressor(s)—which will, in turn, help you to control your stress.

Practice the Three P's: Plan, prioritize, and prepare. There is probably nothing that stimulates a college student's stress level more than the fourth P: procrastination. When given a task, waiting until the last minute to think about how to complete it on time and well simply does not work. All it does is add another layer of stress to the ones most college students are already experiencing. If you can learn to make lists of tasks to be completed, to prioritize those tasks, to place them on your calendar, and to allot yourself the time it takes to prepare and revise presentations, papers or projects, you will do wonders for your stress levels and for your self-esteem. You want to succeed, but you can easily sabotage your attempts to achieve success by letting stress get the better of you as a result of procrastination. While it is true that some of us work well under pressure, it is equally true that none of us can produce our best work if we don't give the three P's their rightful due.

Have A Good Laugh: "There is healing power in laughter," a friend once told me, and I have found this statement to be very true. Whether you use the Sunday comics, a Steve Martin video, or a comedy club, find a way to laugh deeply, to laugh heartily, and to laugh often. It's good for the body, it's good for the spirit, and it's very good for stress reduction, especially because stress often causes us to become overly tense and serious.

Consider Taking A Time-Out: Whether you take a much needed vacation or a leave of absence from school, this "time-out" will go a long way toward helping you "decompress from stress," which will, in turn, help you focus more on your studies. Taking a time-out may also entail eliminating a stressor from your life altogether (e.g., a particular job or a relationship). As I often tell students, it is better to take some time off rather than forever blemish your transcripts with substandard grades or withdrawals. Even if you do take a time-out, you will not actually lose any time since you will eventually have to make up all those substandard grades and withdrawals if you choose to stay in school while under very high stress. The time-out will not affect your employability either. You will still have more time than you need to enjoy your chosen occupation, and you may have a much better chance of getting hired if you have the kind of impressive academic record that a time-out can often help you achieve.

Broaden Your Connections: Since stress can cause depression and anxiety, now is the time to form new connections … to people, to pets, and to nature. Whether you join a new club on campus, engage in community service, or start an internship related to your chosen career, you will be surrounded by people who can distract you from your stressor(s) or offer the support you need to better manage them. Bottling everything up inside rather than seeking the support of others will only intensify your stress. In the same way we need to share our grief when we lose something we love, so, too, do we need to share our troubles when they feel overwhelming to us. Pets provide us with a different kind of support, of course. Their unconditional love and devotion, their calming presence, and their constant antics can both soothe and distract even the most stressed individuals. And, finally, there are the vast expanses of nature in the form of the sea, the stars, and the mountains—to name but a few—that can provide the rest and renewal as well as the more balanced perspective that stressed individuals may very well need. Making the effort to commit to people, to pets, and/ or to nature can be an excellent stress management technique.

Ask Yourself the Five or Ten Year Question: Every so often, just to put everything in perspective with regard to your current stressors, it's not a bad idea to ask what I call the "five or ten year question." To do so, simply think about whatever is most troubling to you and then immediately ask: "In five (or ten) years, is this even going to matter?" Nine times out of ten, your answer will probably be a resounding "No," since there is very little we cannot correct in five or ten years and since what matters to us today often does not matter at all a few years down the road.

Adjust Your Attitude: Since stress is caused by your reaction to an event, this last suggestion for stress management is perhaps the most important of all, but it is probably the most difficult to implement as well. When it comes to stress, you need to remember that what you think can either reduce or increase your stress levels. To this end, keep in mind that most people engage in four types of stress producing thoughts, and the more aware you become of these thought patterns, the better your chances of reducing or eliminating stress. So, from now on, try to catch yourself *filtering* where you "magnify the negative" and "filter out the positive"; *personalizing* where you blame yourself when "something bad occurs"; *catastrophizing* where you "automatically anticipate the worst"; and *polarizing* where you see things as "good or bad" with no in between (Mayo, 2011). All of these thought patterns, which are evidenced in the following statements, can significantly increase your stress levels:

> "My professor said my dance technique was good but that I needed to improve, so I guess I am really a bad dancer."
>
> "It's my fault that my parents are getting a divorce now that I am in college."

"If my boyfriend breaks up with me, I'll never find anyone else."

"I didn't get chosen for this job because I'm not good enough."

Do you see the pattern of negative thinking that makes an already stressful situation—the evaluation of dance abilities, a parental divorce, a broken relationship, or a form of rejection—even more stressful? How much more useful (and accurate) it would have been to replace these negative thoughts with more balanced ones such as these:

> "I am thrilled that my dance technique meets with my professor's approval. All I need to do to improve on it even more is spend some extra time on my routines."

> "I am very sad that my parents are getting divorced, but I understand that they are no longer able to work out their differences."

> "If my relationship ends, it just means that we were not a good match for each other and that I will find someone else who is a much more suitable partner for me."

> "I wish I could have been chosen for this position, but perhaps it was not the best one for my current level of experience and training. As I develop more in these areas, additional opportunities will open up for me."

As you, too, learn to recognize and replace your stress-producing thoughts with stress-reducing ones, you will enjoy a much greater sense of peace and balance in your life, both of which will result in the success you desire to achieve. It's all about learning to talk to yourself in a positive light. Remember that, more often than not, you are frightening yourself with your own thoughts, thereby increasing your stress levels. Deliberately producing more balanced thoughts will go a long way toward ending this self-tyranny once and for all.

One final note with regard to making an "attitude adjustment" applies to any stressor you may encounter and directly relates to your response to it. Always remember that there are only four ways to approach a stressor: you can avoid it, you can alter it, you can adapt to it, or you can accept it (Mayo, 2010). In other words, you can eliminate it (e.g., by quitting a stressful job); you can change it (e.g., by limiting the time you spend with difficult family members); you can adapt to it (e.g., by counting to ten—or fifty—before you respond to a frequently demanding partner); or you can accept it by refusing to let it upset you anymore. In sum, when it comes to making an attitude adjustment, your choice is always to change the situation—if you can—or to change your attitude if you cannot.

Final Remarks

I began this chapter by quoting some of Robert Eliot's words, not just because they tend to elicit smiles from most readers (thereby reducing their stress levels) but because they may well express the best cure for stress that the vast majority of us can ever hope to find. In the end, much of the stress we encounter in our lives results from our reaction to one of the basic facts of life, which has likewise been expressed in a quote by Francois de la Rochefoucauld: "The only thing constant in life is change." The more we attach, the more we cling to what was, and the more we resist what is to be, the greater the stress we will experience. If we wholeheartedly surrender to the present moment by spending less time fighting or fleeing and more time flowing, we could significantly diminish our stress at the same time we markedly enhance our ability to achieve success both in college and in life.

7

When You Try Your Best Without Success:

Understanding Learning Disabilities

The will to succeed is important, but what's even more important is the will to prepare.

--Bobby Knight

Being defeated is often a temporary condition. Giving up is what makes it permanent.

--Marilyn vas Savant

If I were to ask you the following questions, would you answer "Yes" to one or more of them?

- Do you put a lot of time and effort into your schoolwork without achieving the high grades you expect?
- Have you often (or always) struggled with a particular subject such as reading, writing, and/or mathematics?
- As a college student, did you have to take developmental (i.e., pre-collegiate) courses in English and math? If so, did you pass these courses the first time around or did you have to repeat them?

I have often asked the first two questions of students whose transcripts tell a story about their academic performance that they would rather not disclose to anyone. These same students are the ones who are not making what we call "satisfactory academic progress." They may be on academic or progress probation and they may likewise be in jeopardy of losing their financial aid, which is what most often occasions their appointment with me. As a teacher and as a counselor, I have seen hundreds of students who answered "Yes" to the first two questions and whose transcripts answered "Yes" to the third ... many of whom had an undiagnosed learning disability. For years, they struggled in school, concluded they were "stupid," and considered dropping out on a fairly regular basis. If you are one such student, this chapter will help you understand why you, too, have struggled in school as a result of a learning disability. Equally important, you will learn what you can do about your disability before it becomes still another barrier to your success in college and in life.

Defining the Problem: What is a Learning Disability?

According to the National Dissemination Center for Children and Youth With Disabilities (2011), a "learning disability is a general term that describes specific kinds of learning problems" that "can cause a person to have trouble learning and using certain skills," the most common of which are reading, writing, listening, speaking, reasoning, and mathematical computation. On a slightly more technical note, learning disabilities have likewise been defined by the National Center for Learning Disabilities (2013) as "neurological [disorders] that [affect] the brain's ability to receive, process, store and respond to information," all skills that are vital for scholastic success. Because the term "neurological disorder" conjures up images of mental retardation in the minds of some, I want to emphasize at this point that nothing could be further from the truth. If you have a learning disability, you are not mentally retarded, nor are you a "slow learner." In fact, individuals must be of average to above average intelligence to qualify as learning disabled, but there is a noticeable discrepancy between their intelligence and their performance. To this end, I often tell students that I prefer to use the term "learning difference" rather than "disability" because I think it more accurately reflects the true nature of the condition, namely, that certain individuals process information differently (NICHCY, 2011). The distinction between learning disabilities and other conditions leading to low achievement is nicely underscored in the Individuals With Disabilities Act (IDEA) which states that "Learning disabilities do not include … learning problems that are primarily the result of visual, hearing, or motor disabilities, of mental retardation, of emotional disturbance, or of environmental, cultural, or economic disadvantage."

One other myth about learning disabilities that should be dispelled at this point is that they are somehow related to poor motivation. Again, nothing could be further from the truth. A learning disability may affect an individual's motivation levels if he/she repeatedly struggles with a task, but overcoming a learning disability does not result from somehow improving motivation. In fact, individuals with learning disabilities often try far harder to succeed than those without them. The problem is never motivational; the problem is always the disability itself (Horowitz & Golembeski, 2013).

Like every other hidden barrier to college success discussed in this book, learning disabilities can range from mild to severe (NCLD, 2013) and are often divided into four distinct types, each of which is defined below.

Dyslexia: People with dyslexia have trouble processing language, particularly in the areas of reading, writing and spelling.

Dyscalculia: As its name implies, dyscalculia causes individuals to struggle with mathematics. They may experience difficulties with computation as well as remembering formulas and principles.

Dysgraphia: Individuals with dysgraphia have difficulty writing; consequently, their handwriting is often very messy and may be laced with spelling errors.

Dyspraxia: This learning disability causes individuals to struggle with "fine motor skills" that require "coordination and manual dexterity," including buttoning a shirt or drawing (NCLD, 2013).

In addition to the four types of learning disabilities outlined above, some individuals may also suffer from auditory and/or visual processing disorders that likewise make it difficult for them to interpret material that is presented via sight and sound. These disorders can, in turn, negatively affect their learning process as well as their ability to read, write, and compute (NCLD, 2013).

Identifying the Problem: How Do I Know If I Have a Learning Disability?

While affirmative answers to the questions I raise at the outset of this chapter are a start, you may also want to review your entire academic history to determine if the signs listed below correspond to your experiences in school. In addition, you should also consider whether there is a notable discrepancy between your ability and your performance. You will need to be professionally assessed to receive an actual diagnosis, of course, but reflecting upon the material below should help you to ascertain whether or not you would benefit from this type of an assessment.

If you do, in fact, have a learning disability, your academic history may include difficulty performing a number of the following tasks:

- Learning the alphabet, rhyming words, or connecting letters to sounds
- Reading aloud without making numerous mistakes
- Comprehending written material
- Spelling correctly
- Writing neatly or holding a pencil with ease
- Explaining ideas in writing
- Learning language in a timely manner and/or acquiring a broad vocabulary
- Remembering the sounds letters make and/or hearing slight differences between words
- Understanding jokes, comic strips, and sarcasm
- Following directions
- Pronouncing words or correctly using similarly sounding words
- Organizing spoken or written material
- Following the social rules of conversation, such as taking turns or standing an appropriate distance from a speaker
- Re-telling a story in order
- Knowing where to begin a task or how to continue it
- Not confusing math symbols and/or correctly reading numbers (NICHCY, 2011).

If I were to summarize these common signs of learning disabilities, I would simply say "difficulty listening, speaking, reading, writing and/or computing." Since individuals are born with learning disabilities, I would preface this summary with the words "a history of"—even if the disability is not formally diagnosed until much later in life.

One other point to keep in mind is that approximately one third of people with learning disabilities also have Attention Deficit Hyperactivity Disorder (ADHD), a condition that makes it difficult to concentrate, sit still, delay gratification and control impulses (NCLD, 2013). So, if you know you have ADHD, you may also have a learning disability as well—and vice versa.

Discovering that you have a learning disability can be both unsettling and liberating. You may initially find your newly diagnosed condition troubling because you haven't yet learned how to manage it, but you will also find it liberating—as so many of my students do—because you will finally understand why you have struggled for so long to achieve success in school. With your formal diagnosis will come a host of valuable resources to help you succeed.

Understanding the Problem: What Causes Learning Disabilities?

When I was a teaching credential candidate, I took a course designed for special educators, and when I began work on my counseling degree, I also took a graduate level course that focused on students with learning disabilities/differences. In both of these courses, I was told that no one really knows what causes learning disabilities. A number of possible causes have been identified, but none has proven to be the definitive cause. Possible causes of learning disabilities include heredity, prenatal or birthing complications, and post-birth problems (NCLD, 2013). With regard to heredity, researchers have seen that learning disabilities do tend to run in families, a reality I have myself observed. Prenatal or birthing complications might include, for example, "drug or alcohol use during pregnancy, low birth weight, lack of oxygen, and premature or prolonged labor" (NCLD, 2013). Finally, post birthing problems including "head injuries, poor nutrition, and exposure to toxic substances such as lead" may also cause learning disabilities (NCLD, 2013).

Other more controversial theories concerning the causes of learning disabilities have been proposed, but nothing has been proven in this regard, and therapies targeting these areas have not yielded any meaningful results. The most we can safely say is that "learning disabilities are caused by differences in how a person's brain works and how it processes information," (NICHCY, 2011), but what, exactly, causes these particular differences is, in all probability, specific to the individuals who have them.

What we do know with absolute certainty is that "learning disabilities are not caused by economic disadvantage, environmental factors or cultural differences" (NCLD, 2013).

When compared to many of the other hidden barriers to college success discussed in this book, understanding causes is not really that important insofar as nothing you are feeling or experiencing (or choosing not to feel or experience) is a contributing factor to your learning difference. Put another way, you are not causing your own problem, nor are you exacerbating it. Given that learning disabilities often cause students a great deal of distress in the form of self-blame, self-doubt, or self-deprecating thoughts, your choice to internalize that you are not, in fact, responsible for your own learning challenges may go a long way toward helping you effectively address them.

Solving the Problem: Pathways to Managing Learning Disabilities

I have substituted the word "managing" for "healing" in the subtitle above because there is no "cure" for a learning disability. In other words, you cannot take medication, elect to have surgery, or discontinue a certain behavior in order to heal. What you can do, however, is to start by acknowledging that your brain does, in fact, process information differently and then you can learn how to access and skillfully employ the strategies that will prevent your learning disability from becoming an intransigent barrier to your success as a college student. This particular learning process involves a number of specific steps, each of which is discussed below.

Step 1: Identify the Problem

If you already know that you have a learning disability, you can skip this step. However, as both a teacher and as a counselor, it has been my experience that many college students do not find out they have a specific learning disability until they are in college. Yes, they have always struggled in school, but for any number of reasons, ranging from "social promotion" to teachers who may not have been entirely committed to the success of all of their pupils, these same students enter college expecting to struggle yet still succeed. Instead, they start to fail their courses ... even when they have been placed in remedial English and math. In this first step, I am suggesting that you closely examine your own academic history—past and present. Do you see a pattern? Are you struggling to pass your college courses and do your challenges seem to be influenced by your abilities in the areas of reading, writing and/or computation? If you believe you do, in fact, have a problem, your first step is to get tested. Some colleges or universities will provide this testing free of charge through their offices for students with disabilities. If they do not, you will need to be tested privately since your college will require documentation in order to provide you with the accommodations that will help you succeed. You can find qualified testing professionals via the National Center for Learning Disabilities (www.ncld.org). A word of warning: private assessments are not cheap, but they are well worth it in the long run since it may be difficult, if not impossible, for students with learning disabilities to succeed in college without certain accommodations.

Step 2: Know Your Rights and Responsibilities

Once you discover that you do, in fact, have a learning disability, keep in mind that your desire to seek assistance for it is not just something you wish to do; it is also your right. As college students, you are protected by both the American With Disabilities Act (ADA) and Section 504 of the Rehabilitation Act of 1973 (NCLD, 2013). These civil rights laws "require that colleges provide [learning disabled students] access to [reasonable] accommodations … and afford them an 'equal opportunity' in the institution's programs, activities, and services" (Rabinovitz, 2011). To be reasonable, the accommodations may not include anything that "requires significant alteration to the program or activity; results in the lowering of academic or technical standards; or causes the college to incur undue financial hardship" (Rabinovitz, 2011). In order to receive these accommodations, it is your responsibility to provide your college or university with documentation to verify your disability. Colleges and universities establish their own requirements for documentation in terms of its timeliness and format (Rabinovitz, 2011), so you will need to ascertain what your college or university requires before you submit anything to them.

Step 3: Access the Resources You May Need

Not every student with a learning disability will need all of the services discussed on the following pages, of course. I am merely providing a representative sample of the types of support services that often prove quite useful to students with learning challenges.

Offices for Students With Disabilities: This office is where you will need to begin. While it is true that colleges and universities are required by law to provide assistance to students with disabilities, you may still need to be your own best advocate by understanding your rights and working with others to ensure that you receive the accommodations to which you are legally entitled. Such accommodations might, for example, include un-timed tests, longer periods of time to complete assignments, note-takers, and access to a variety of assistive technologies, including "tape recorders, talking calculators, screen readers that read aloud Internet articles and electronic text documents ... or Personal Digital Assistants (PDA's) that can help you organize your daily activities and assignments" (Rabinovitz, 2011)—to name but a few. Though they may not sound like much, oftentimes these simple accommodations are what enable a learning disabled student to achieve success in college. Aside from providing you with reasonable accommodations, your college or university's office for students with disabilities can also offer (or refer you to) a number of the additional resources that are described below.

Tutorial Services: Every campus offers some form of tutorial support for all students, not just those with learning disabilities. Depending upon your campus, these services may be offered through individual departments (e.g., English or math), tutorial centers, the library's Learning Resource Center, and/or via individual programs, including those for disabled students. It is, of course, also possible to hire a private tutor, but that can get very costly if you need tutoring on a weekly basis. Given how readily available tutoring services are on most college campuses, it is surprising how many students neglect to access them until it is too late. I recommend including tutoring in your weekly schedule so that you will commit to it just as you would for a class that meets every week.

Academic Strategies or Personal/Human Development Courses: In addition to tutoring services, many campuses also offer courses to enhance their students' success in college. Course topics can include time management, improving memory and concentration, test taking-strategies, and study skills such as note-taking. All of these courses can prove very beneficial to learning disabled students and should not be discounted merely because they do not lead to a degree. Though they do not afford students degree credit, the skills they cover may very well make it possible for numerous students, including those with learning challenges, to achieve their goals.

Educate Yourself: This chapter only skims the surface of a very complex topic. Ultimately, it's up to you to learn about your disability and how it may affect your academic, professional and personal life. You'll also want to explore the learning strategies that work best for you and you'll need to discover how to capitalize on your strengths and how to minimize your challenges. Numerous books have been written on the topic of learning disabilities, but you may also find the following organizations helpful:

International Dyslexia Association
www.interdys.org

Learning Disabilities Association of America
www.ldanatl.org

National Center for Learning Disabilities
www.ncld.org

Get to Know Your Professors: This piece of advice is one I would share with all students, regardless of whether or not they have a learning disability. However, I believe it is particularly important for students with learning challenges to connect with their professors. If you do not understand some of the material that is being presented in class, make it a point to talk to your professor. He or she may be able to provide you with some additional resource material that could prove very useful to you. Professors will also tend to take more of an interest in students who seem committed to learning, so make it a point to show your professors that you are one such student. Once they see that you are not there about a grade but because you desire to truly grasp the material they are presenting, you will have created for yourself a very valuable resource … and, perhaps, a lifelong one as well.

Counseling: Learning disabilities can stir up a whole host of additional issues for students, ranging from stress to low self-esteem. These issues may become more of a barrier to college success than the disability itself if they are not properly managed. Working with a counselor can help you address any issue your disability may have engendered for you. In addition to processing the feelings associated with your disability, counseling therapy can also provide you with some excellent coping strategies that you can successfully employ in your academic, professional, and personal lives.

Join (Or Start) a Support Group for Students With Learning Disabilities: All of the benefits of support groups that I have discussed in previous chapters apply to students with learning disabilities as well. Not only will you be vastly relieved to find that others share your learning challenges but you will also acquire a number of valuable techniques for academic success that you can readily apply. When it comes to learning disabilities, there is no reason to cope with them alone, especially when they affect so many students. In other words, you don't have to "reinvent the wheel" to manage your own disability; you can build upon the successes of others who have traveled the road before you at the same time you garner the support you need to stay focused, motivated, and committed.

Following these three simple steps— identifying the problem, knowing your rights and responsibilities, and accessing the resources you may need—will go a long way toward transforming what could be a formidable barrier into a learning challenge that is actually quite manageable … despite its lifelong nature.

Final Remarks

Taped to my desk at work in full view of my students is a picture that depicts a frog being consumed by a pelican. There is only one hitch: the frog has managed to wrap his hands around the bird's neck and is in the process of strangling it. Etched above this picture are the words: "NEVER Give Up!" If I could offer one piece of advice to all of my learning disabled students, these very words are the ones I would choose to use. There will be many, many times when you want to give up. Indeed, a significant number of your classmates have already done so and never even made it to college. But you did, and now that you are here, you can begin to see, perhaps for the first time ever, that it is not too late to get the help you need and that your learning disability is not really that different from all the other challenges people face when they are trying to reach a goal. Every student reading this book has dealt with or is dealing with at least one of the barriers to college success that I have discussed in previous chapters. The only real difference between them and you is the nature of the barrier you each face. What is far, far more important, however, is what you all share in common: the determination to succeed and the willingness to make the effort. With these very valuable resources in hand, nothing, not even a learning disability, can hold you back. So, I say to each of you: Don't give up, even when it seems like you are facing odds that you just can't beat. You can and you will succeed … with a little patience, a lot of perseverance, and, like the frog in my picture, some very strong hands around the neck of your own self-doubt.

8

When You Think You're Just Not Good Enough:

Understanding Self-Esteem

No one can make you feel inferior without your consent.
--Eleanor Roosevelt

We have to learn to be our own best friends because we fall
too easily into the trap of being our own worst enemies.
--Roderick Thorpe

Every chapter in this book is about making a choice: the choice to admit you have a problem and the choice to do something about it. For this reason, I have saved the most important choice you will make as a college student for the final chapter of this book. It is the choice that will, in large part, determine whether or not you struggle to overcome one or more of the aforementioned hidden barriers to college success … and for how long. Put simply, it is the choice to believe in yourself and in your inherent potential as a human being or to let other people and/or social and cultural messages define and limit who you are and what you can and cannot do. I am, of course, talking about self-esteem, both positive and negative. Because it is the latter that constitutes such a significant barrier to college success, however, I will primarily focus this chapter on how low self-esteem can so easily prevent you from achieving your goals—or even making an attempt to do so—and what, specifically, you can do about it.

Defining the Problem: What is Self-Esteem?

Simply put, self-esteem refers to what you think and how you feel about yourself, inclusive of your skills and abilities, your personality, your character, and, of course, your physical appearance. It is an enormously powerful factor in your life, influencing the nature and number of your relationships, your academic and professional performance, your choice of occupation, and any other lifestyle choices you make. How you think, how you feel, and how you behave are all profoundly affected by your self-esteem. Because self-esteem is "emotional, evaluative, and cognitive" (Reasoner, 2010), it causes us to think certain thoughts and to experience a wide range of feelings. In the case of low self-esteem, thoughts are primarily self-limiting and feelings are predominantly negative, ranging from shame to depression.

In general, individuals with positive self-esteem typically like themselves, regardless of what they have or have not accomplished in life and regardless of anything others say or do to them. In contrast, those with low self-esteem do not love (or even like) themselves, they are extremely self-critical, and they tend to define themselves based on what they have or have not accomplished and/or on how others treat them. No matter what they do or how much they achieve, however, deep down inside, all individuals with low self-esteem believe is that they are not—or that they will never be—good enough, smart enough, talented enough or enough of any other positive quality they can name.

As you will see on the following pages, a key difference between positive and negative self-esteem relates to whether you define yourself internally or externally. In other words, you either define self-esteem from within by recognizing and affirming the true nature of your authentic self or you define it externally with regard to how other people respond to you and/or with respect to what you have or have not achieved (e.g., money, fame, power, and so forth). Equally important, you also externally define your self-esteem using the interpretive stories you have told yourself about what other people's responses to you mean and about what your "failures" and mistakes in life mean. When it comes to healing low self-esteem, a critical component in the healing process is to reject these stories based on external circumstances and replace them with the truth about who you are. To do so most effectively, you will need to consider the causes of low self-esteem, many of which are highlighted later in this chapter.

Identifying the Problem: How Do I Know If I Have Low Self-Esteem?

There are many online self-esteem assessments you can take, but I usually recommend that students begin with the following exercise: Write the words "I am" on a sheet of paper and then list all the words and phrases that come to mind—without censoring yourself in any way. Remember: No one but you is going to see this list. So, for example, you might find yourself generating words like smart, ugly, a failure, an awesome basketball player, a loving mother (or father), uncoordinated, a graceful dancer, and so forth. If your list is primarily positive, you may have high self-esteem, and if it is primarily negative, your self-esteem is probably low. I also recommend asking yourself if you love (or even like) yourself and then writing down whatever comes to mind in response to that question. That, too, should give you an idea of whether your self-esteem is high or low.

Aside from these very simple exercises (or any more detailed assessment you may take), there are also a number of personal characteristics associated with low self-esteem, including de-valuing your "opinions or ideas" as well as your talents and abilities, focusing "on your perceived weaknesses and faults," believing that "others are more capable or successful than you are," being "unable to accept compliments or positive feedback," and fearing failure "which can hold you back from succeeding [at] work or [in] school" (Mayo, 2011). Individuals with low self-esteem are also more likely to develop "eating disorders, addictions, depression and anxiety" (Mayo, 2011).

Not a pretty picture, is it? That's the bad news. The good news is that low self-esteem is not a life sentence. You *can* change how you view yourself, thereby reversing the negative effects low self-worth may have had (or is having) on your life, but first, you need to understand what has caused you to develop such a low regard for self, and it is to this very topic that we will now turn our attention.

Understanding the Problem: What Causes Low Self-Esteem?

I like to refer to the creation of self-esteem as a "developmental process" because it does indeed develop and change over time, though its origin is both genetic and environmental. With regard to the former, if you peruse the National Institutes of Health public access documents, you will indeed find studies that support a genetic link to self-esteem. This scientific evidence notwithstanding, however, if you were to likewise take the time to observe babies or young children, you would notice that they typically manifest many of the qualities associated with high self-esteem—sometimes to their detriment! There is nothing they cannot do and no risk they will not take in their desire to explore, to create, and to achieve whatever little goals they have set for themselves. So, aside from genetics, why does this happy, courageous, inquisitive, carefree, confident little soul eventually lose these essentially self-affirming qualities? The answer to that question is fairly complex, but for our purposes in this book, I am going to simplify it with the oft-quoted phrase: "Life happens."

When we are very young, we may be naturally confident and courageous, but we are also utterly dependent upon others for our own survival and, to a great extent, for our own sense of self-worth as well. If we are made to feel loved and valued when we are young, we have a much better chance of developing positive self-esteem than we do if we are made to feel unloved or worthless (Mayo, 2011). The messages we receive while we are still young and vulnerable—both verbal and non-verbal—as well as our interpretation of them significantly contribute to the development of our self-esteem, positive or negative. These messages come from a variety of sources, including "parents, siblings, peers, teachers, and other important contacts" (Mayo, 2011). They also come in a variety of forms, such as looks, harsh words, physical assaults, or even neglect. A look of love or a kind word can contribute to our sense of being lovable just as an abusive act or harsh criticism can contribute to our sense of worthlessness. After all, how can someone be valuable or lovable if he is constantly told how stupid he is or if she is beaten or used for someone else's pleasure? Regrettably, during this critical developmental stage, we are too young to understand and internalize that nothing anyone says or does to us can diminish our essential value or in any way limit what we can achieve in life. Instead, we internalize the negative messages we receive, and they become an integral part of our developing sense of self.

As we grow older, social and cultural messages can reinforce or alter our self-esteem. If we perceive that certain characteristics are valued in our society (e.g., wealth or a slim figure) and we do not happen to possess these characteristics, our self-esteem can also suffer, especially if this supposed lack is brought to our attention by others.

As we grow still older, our perception of not being good enough is reinforced by the competitive nature of our academic and professional experiences. We quickly learn that our worth is measured not by who we are but by what we do, how many degrees we possess, how much money we make, what kind of car we drive, where we live, what labels we wear on our clothing, and so forth. In fact, as adults, the two most common questions we may be asked are: "What do you do?" and "Where do you live?"

We inadvertently contribute to this problem with our own feelings of worthlessness. Suddenly, life isn't about exploring or joyfully creating anymore—it's about proving we are good enough, and we will go to any lengths to do so, all the while losing our true selves in the process. Because we were not made to feel loved or valued early on, all of our vital energy is spent trying to gain the love and approval we never received. If that means starving ourselves to death as anorexics, we do it. If that means skipping class to be part of the "in crowd," we do it. If that means drinking or using to the point of excess just to belong to a fraternity, we do it. Or, if that means risking an unplanned pregnancy to feel "loved," we do it. No matter what it takes or how much we have to sacrifice, we do it … anything is better than continuing to harbor feelings of worthlessness, rejection, and self-loathing.

As I have observed firsthand, we may also inadvertently contribute to the problem of low self-esteem by setting unrealistic goals for ourselves. If, for example, we think the only way to be "good enough" is to earn a medical degree but we do not happen to be gifted in the areas of math or science, then we are, of course, setting ourselves up not only for a possible failure but also for the self-recriminations that will undoubtedly accompany this failure. If we have low self-esteem, all of our experiences with "failures" or mistakes can serve to exacerbate the problem. To experience success and thus promote positive self-esteem, we need to realistically assess our gifts and talents, an oftentimes challenging task for individuals with low self-esteem—but, as you will shortly see, not an impossible one.

On the subject of success and failure, our experience of either one also contributes to our sense of self. If we predominantly experience success and if we are in the process of developing positive self-esteem, each success will reinforce our sense of self-worth. If, on the other hand, we primarily experience failures, perhaps because the authority figures in our lives are asking too much of us, or if our perfectly natural failures/ mistakes are met with harsh criticism, we are far more likely to develop a negative regard for self. We may also consider any type of loss (e.g., a relationship, a job or money) as a personal failure on our part, and that, too, can diminish our self-esteem.

Because I have referred to the creation of self-esteem as a "developmental process" and because this book has been written for college students, I want to close our discussion of causes with the observation that our college years also contribute to the quality of our self-esteem. Giving what our professors clearly perceive as the "wrong" answer in class, fitting in with peers either in class or in the dorm, negotiating romantic relationships, and meeting higher academic standards—to name but a few of the pressures college students face—can also influence and/or reinforce our developing sense of self ... depending upon how we handle each new challenge with which we are faced.

Solving the Problem: Pathways to Improving Self-Esteem

There are a variety of proven techniques you can employ on your own to improve your self-esteem, but I do recommend a couple of professional resources for those of you whose self-esteem is particularly low, so much so that it is interfering with your ability to achieve success, and I also recommend these professional resources for those of you whose low self-esteem has caused or has resulted from one of the other hidden barriers to college success discussed in this book.

Asking for Help

If you decide to seek professional help for low self-esteem, I would recommend the following resources:

Individual or Group Counseling: Because issues with low self-esteem often result from family dynamics, childhood traumas, or significant losses, electing to process these events with a licensed therapist will help you begin to separate whatever was said or done to you from who you are. More often than not, whatever happened was about something over which you had little or no control. We cannot, after all, choose our parents, nor can we mandate how it is we need them to treat us. We get what we get. In the same way, we cannot control our spouse's desire to pursue someone else, the stock market crash that caused us to lose a significant amount of money, or the economic downturn that led to the loss of our job. And, even if we incurred a loss for which we were somehow responsible, individual or group counseling can help us learn to forgive ourselves, accept our own humanity with all its limitations, change our behavior (if necessary) and move on. Finally, individual or group counseling can also be an excellent arena for experimenting with some of the self-help techniques described below.

Self-Esteem Seminars and Workshops: You may be able to find this particular resource at your college or university's health center. Very often, such centers employ school psychologists who facilitate workshops or support groups for students struggling with some of the barriers to college success discussed in this book, including low self-esteem. Colleges and universities may also offer seminars on these topics via their community education programs.

Medical Treatment: While there is obviously no drug for individuals suffering from low self-esteem, there are medical treatments for those of you whose self-esteem has caused or has resulted from some of the other hidden barriers to college success about which you have already read, including depression, anxiety, addictions, and eating disorders. If you are, in fact, struggling with these issues as well, I would encourage you to consult your healthcare professional to explore treatment options from which you might benefit along with the other professional resources and self-help techniques provided in the foregoing chapters.

Learning to Help Yourself

Even if you seek professional help in resolving your self-esteem issues, you are still your own best resource in this area since you are the only one who is with yourself 24/7 and only you can control how you react to whatever happens in your life. To this end, you may find a number of the following strategies very useful if you commit to practicing them consistently and conscientiously. I have not listed them in any particular order, so feel free to pick and choose those you find most appealing.

> *Talk Back to Your Inner Critic:* Since "your own thoughts have perhaps the biggest impact on self-esteem" (Mayo, 2011), one of the best ways to improve it is by employing the Cognitive Behavioral Therapy (CBT) technique I discussed in Chapters 1 and 2. Again, this strategy requires that you negate or positively restate every negative thought you have about yourself, your abilities, or your potential. So, for example, if you find yourself thinking, "I am too stupid to pass my English class," you would instead say: "I am every bit as intelligent as my other classmates, all of whom placed into this class right alongside me, and if I study hard, do my best, and seek the assistance of a tutor, I will pass this class." For CBT to be truly effective, you must employ it *every* time you have a negative thought. Only by so doing will you begin to see that just because you have a thought does not mean it is a *true* thought. Conscientiously employing the CBT technique will help you learn to generate consistently true thoughts that will, in turn, enhance your self-esteem and positively influence your mood. Stated another way, once you stop putting yourself down, the only way to go is up.

> *Create and Practice Using Affirmations:* Affirmations can be employed right alongside your CBT techniques. The only difference is that you do not wait for negative thoughts to arise

before you employ this strategy. You simply make positive statements about yourself throughout the day. So, for example, you might say "I am worthy of respect" while brushing your teeth in the morning or "I have a great personality and people genuinely like me" while you are doing the dishes or "I handled that conflict with my partner really well today" before going to bed. As "corny" as this technique sounds, it can also be highly effective. Why? Because every time you affirm yourself with loving words and thoughts, you are negating your early experiences of criticism and rejection, thereby stripping them of the power they hold over you.

Do It Scared: Because individuals with low self-esteem are so afraid of failure, they often don't step outside of their rigidly controlled comfort zone where they are sure not to "fail," thereby lowering their self-esteem even further. Thus, "doing it scared" can produce life-changing results for two very important reasons. First, as I frequently tell students, those who shoot for something very often get it, and those who shoot for nothing get that too. Secondly, as the old adage says, "You never know until you try." Taken together, these two reasons underscore a very important fact of life: You will never discover what it is you excel at or enjoy doing if you don't take action … no matter how scared you are and no matter how strongly your inner critic is discouraging you in this regard. As every great inventor knows, the road to success is paved with a fair share of "failures," but each one was actually a necessary prerequisite to success. When you feel fear at the prospect of trying something new or if your inner critic discourages you in this endeavor, ask yourself this question: "What's the worst thing that will happen if I fail?" Then compare your answer to this question: "What's the worst thing that will happen if I don't even try?" I think you'll find that your answer to the second question is far more dissuasive than is your answer to the first—unless, of course, you really do not want to succeed in life. On that note, please remember that it's all right to take baby steps. Even baby steps will serve to raise your self-esteem because at least you are doing something to change rather than nothing at all.

Rewrite Your Story: As noted earlier, everybody has a story and everybody has a story about him or herself based on that story. The story might go something like this: "My father beat me, told me I would never amount to anything, and refused to help pay for my college education. That must mean I'm not lovable, I'm not capable, and I'm not worth investing in." That's a very powerful message to create and internalize based on past life experiences, and, if left unchallenged, it will most assuredly sabotage this individual's chances of achieving success in his relationships, on his job, and in school. The only way to counter the effects of this story and its interpretation is to rewrite it with objective factual statements. Concretely, this means recognizing and internalizing that you are not what happened to you. In other words, you are not your so-called failures or mistakes. You are not unlovable even if someone did not love you, you are not ugly even if you do not reflect society's standards of "beauty," and you are not a reject even if someone rejected or abandoned you. There are many other examples of this concept I could give you, but all of them boil down to one simple truth: You are not your past experience and you are not your interpretation of it. So, how do you counter this tendency to define yourself based on what has happened to you? I suggest that you write your "story" and then rewrite it with a series of "I am not ..." statements. Thereafter, LET IT GO and commit to living in the present moment as who you really are ... a worthy, lovable, capable, accomplished expression of life. There is no need to revisit the past or cling to the interpretations it may have generated for you. You will not find your true self in your past. You will only ever find it in the present moment in the form of a truly remarkable being who has, for better or worse, experienced—but not been destroyed by—some of life's most challenging slings and arrows.

Honor the Four Agreements: If you have not yet read Don Miguel Ruiz' (1997) book The Four Agreements, now might be a good time to do so. In this book, he discusses four ancient but still very relevant Toltec teachings: (1) Do not speak ill of others or yourself; (2) Do not take anything personally; (3) Do not make assumptions; and (4) Always do your best. Being mindful of all four teachings can serve to enhance your self-esteem. I have already discussed how to talk about yourself but extending the same courtesy to others will raise your self-esteem as well since, deep down inside, we all know it is unkind to gossip about or criticize other people, and it's hard to feel good about ourselves when we are being unkind. Not taking anything personally by remaining immune to the bad (or good) opinion of others is also very good advice. The point is to separate what others say about you from who you really are at the same time you do not depend upon what others think of you to measure your self-worth. With regard to assumptions, if you have low self-esteem, you will always assume that someone intentionally hurt you. Don't. Such assumptions only serve to make you feel even worse about yourself. Nine times out of ten, how the person involved spoke or acted had nothing to do with you at all. Finally, doing your best is always a self-esteem booster. Why? Because we tend to beat ourselves up the most when we know we could have done better with a little more time and effort.

Find the Courage to Change: If there is a particular quality about yourself that you don't like, consider changing it. For example, if you tend to judge or criticize others a lot, stop doing it altogether or stop doing it as soon as you catch yourself in the act. Try complimenting or seeing the good in others instead. Eventually, your old bad habit will be replaced with a new good one—even if you have to "fake it 'til you make it" for awhile.

Look Within: When it comes to enhancing your self-esteem, the worst place to start is outside yourself. As I state at the outset of this chapter, no one and nothing can diminish who you are or what you can accomplish in life. If you rely on external factors to validate your worth as a human being, you are destined to fail, and that is because nothing outside yourself lasts. People who say they love you come and go; compliments are forgotten (or retracted) over time; jobs can be lost and fortunes diminished; trusted friends can become bitter enemies or arch rivals. If you rely on other people and status symbols for your sense of self-worth, where will you be if you lose them? The only way to find and preserve your true self-worth is to look within where you will discover the unique gifts that make you who you are. Do you have a good heart? Are you compassionate? Do you have a gift for motivating, leading or guiding others? Are you ethical? Are you able to make others laugh—even when they would rather cry? These essential qualities are ones no one can destroy—unless you choose to give them that kind of power over you. If you really want to build your self-esteem, take that power back and commit to honoring and cherishing all that you find within. As part of this process, constantly affirm that you are not what you do, you are not what you own, you are not what other people think of you, and you are not your physical appearance. Again, you are that which you will only find deep, deep within.

Learn to Be Your Own Best Friend: If you have low self-esteem, this technique will require some effort on your part. Being your own best friend does not just mean speaking kindly to yourself; it also means treating yourself kindly by eating healthfully, exercising your body, asserting your needs (especially when they are in conflict with the needs of others), daring to put yourself first at times, and allowing yourself to indulge in enjoyable activities, such as a warm bath or a massage. If you have low self-esteem, you tend to treat yourself badly because you don't believe you are worth treating well. Not so! You are as worthy as anyone else on this planet and you, too, deserve to be treated well. Once you begin taking care of yourself in this way, you will likewise begin feeling better about yourself.

Don't Let Others Mistreat You: Part of being your own best friend by taking care of yourself is making sure that others take care of you in loving ways as well. You aren't being loved and valued if you are being emotionally, physically, or verbally abused ... no matter how much or how often your family members, partners, or friends tell you otherwise. The longer you stay in these types of destructive relationships, the harder it is to leave and the more devastating the effects on your self-esteem. Not only is another person demeaning you but you yourself begin to feel like a failure because you are too afraid to leave. Don't do that to yourself. Follow the advice I gave you earlier—do it scared and walk away. Surround yourself with loving, supportive people and inspiring role models. They are the ones who will help you rediscover your hidden treasure ... the authentic and eminently valuable person that you are and that you were born to be.

Ask the "What Is That to Thou?" Question: Would you like to know one of the quickest ways to improve self-esteem? Well, here it is in one simple sentence: Ignore what everybody else is doing or possesses. If you don't do what they do or you don't have what they have, you will start feeling badly about yourself by way of comparison. Every time you are even tempted to compare, ask yourself the biblical question: "What is that to thou?— even if you are not religious. It's just another way of saying to keep your eyes focused on your own life. Everyone is on a journey and you have no idea what anyone else's journey is all about, so focus exclusively on the road you are traveling and make it the best it can be.

Connect to Your Higher Power: If you are so inclined, it can be very helpful to frequently remind yourself that you are loved, honored and cherished by something greater than all the people who have come in and out of your life. This Higher Power could be called God or the Universe or whatever you want it to be. The point is to see yourself as part of something greater ... a valuable, indispensable part ... kind of like the parts of a car. Each one is needed for the car to run and to provide its owner with an enjoyable driving experience. In the same way, connecting to your Higher Power through prayer or meditation or whatever other means you choose can serve as a powerful reminder that you, too, are needed to contribute to the running of the world and to provide others with enjoyment ... not because of anything you do or have but simply because of *who you are.* Put another way, *you matter*—regardless of what anyone else has said or done to you.

Serve: I have mentioned the value of community service in several other chapters, primarily because it is a natural self-esteem booster and can therefore relieve feelings of depression and anxiety. Helping others makes you feel good about yourself and that is because, as human beings, we are programmed to live in community and to help each other out. It is the most natural thing in the world to reach out to help others and quite unnatural to harm them—even if the nightly news or your own life experience would seem to prove otherwise. Doing what comes naturally by serving others will go a long way toward helping you feel better about yourself at the same time you discover and explore who you really are apart from your grades, your job, your car, where you live or any of the other external measures you use to define yourself and your worth as a human being.

Set Goals You Can Achieve By Assessing Your Strengths: The idea behind this last self-esteem booster is to set yourself up for success— not failure—by honestly examining your strengths and challenges so you can focus your efforts on something that comes naturally to you. Whatever it is—fixing cars, writing poetry, cooking or solving mathematical equations—is valuable and worthy of your time and effort, no matter what society may say. If you don't need a degree but can support yourself doing it, then do it. It's about finding what you love to do and what you do well and then doing it passionately. People who have high self-esteem do just that ... regardless of what others think or of what our society says. When all is said and done, that's all that will make you truly happy, and truly happy people tend to have high self-esteem. So, start exploring now while you are still young—even if it means you have to "do it scared." The pay off is priceless and the rewards innumerable.

Final Remarks

In the end, improving self-esteem is about growing up. When we are children, we must let others direct and define us. We don't have a choice in the matter. As adults, however, we direct our own actions and must learn to define ourselves quite apart from our past experiences or any other external factors with which we could measure our self-worth. Achieving a healthy respect for self and an unshakable belief in our inherent value is part and parcel of becoming a mature human being. As is the case with all the other hidden barriers to college success discussed in this book, the choice is yours to make: You can let others define and limit you, thereby forfeiting most (if not all) of your power as a human being to grow and to achieve your goals, or you can look within and celebrate the gifts you find there every day. To continue to define yourself based on past experiences or present (but oftentimes fleeting) status symbols is to rob yourself of the joy that is born once you discover your authentic self—the self no one and nothing can define or limit in any way ... and the *only* self that will enable you to achieve success in college and in life.

CONCLUSION

Free At Last

Just because you find something difficult to do,
don't think that it's humanly impossible.
If something is humanly possible and appropriate,
believe that it can also be attained by you.

--Marcus Aurelius

If I were to ask you to name a central theme that underscores every chapter in this book, it probably wouldn't take you long to identify it as "the choice to be free." In the end, every hidden barrier to college success is about freedom of choice. While it is true that we cannot control many of the external circumstances in our lives, such as the loss of a loved one, child abuse, or having a learning difference, we *can* control our reactions to these circumstances before they begin to control us. No one is consigned to remaining forever lost in a quagmire of depression, anxiety, grief, addictive behaviors, physical or emotional stress, learned helplessness, or self-deprecating thoughts or behaviors. Once we become aware of what is happening in our lives by reading books like this one, we are faced with a clear choice: to remain imprisoned or to set ourselves free. If we truly wish to pursue the goals we entered college to achieve, then the choice to break free of whatever is holding us back is the only logical choice we can make. This book has given you some of the tools you will need to begin your journey toward freedom and success. While I can't promise you that it will be easy to heal, given the nature and scope of the barrier(s) you may need to confront, I *can* promise you that when all is said and done, you will not only achieve the goals you set for yourself as a college student but you will also discover that a completely new life awaits you, a life in which you feel deeply fulfilled, richly blessed and wholly free.

I wish you well on the journey.

Cheryl Kroll
January 2013

APPENDIX

My Personal Plan for Healing

Because creating a specific plan often helps us to commit to its implementation, carefully completing the following exercise should assist you in overcoming your hidden barrier(s) to college success.

Defining the Problem
In the space provided, jot down your hidden barrier(s) to college success.

_____

_____

_____

_____

Identifying the Problem
What specific "symptoms" have led you to conclude that you are, in fact, facing this hidden barrier to college success?

_____

_____

_____

_____

How have these "symptoms" affected your ability to complete your assignments and/or your courses? In other words, how have they affected your ability to reach the academic goals you have set for yourself?

_____

_____

_____

_____

_____

_____

_____

Exploring Causes

Given your family history and/or your life experience, why do you believe you are facing this particular barrier (or these barriers) to college success?

_____

_____

_____

_____

_____

_____

_____

_____

_____

_____

Solving the Problem

As you reflect upon your answer to the foregoing questions, try to identify some professional resources you might consult to help you overcome your hidden barrier(s). When and how do you plan to consult these resources?

Resources I Can Consult:

_____

_____

_____

_____

When and How I Can Access These Resources:

_____

_____

What specific self-help strategies discussed in this book do you think you could also implement? When do you plan to begin using them?

Self-Help Strategies I Can Employ:

_____

_____

_____

_____

When I Plan to Use Them:

_____

_____

Free At Last

This final exercise, which I have adapted from Lucia Capacchione's (2000) book <u>Visioning: Ten Steps to Designing the Life of Your Dreams</u>, is a very powerful and effective one if you actually complete it. Start by envisioning what your life would look like if you were not facing any hidden barriers to success ... either in college or in life. In other words, create a very detailed image in your mind of what success looks like for you. Next, begin to gather pictures from magazines or advertisements or even personal photos that depict your images of success. For example, if you envisioned being a loving and caring parent, then find a picture of someone exhibiting this behavior. Once you have collected these pictures, buy a poster board to design a "success collage." You can start by placing the title of your collage in the center of your poster board. You might, for example, call it "My Successful Life" or "My Vision of Success." Then draw lines out from the center of your title and paste the various pictures that represent your definition of success at the end of each line. At the bottom of the poster, write a personal affirmation that communicates your sincere intention to achieve the vision you have created. For example, you might say: "If you can believe it, you can achieve it. I believe in the vision of success I have created, and I will achieve it." Now post this collage in a strategic location at home and, at least once a day, repeat your success affirmation to yourself as you mentally commit to achieving each goal your pictures represent.

"Visioning" your future in this fashion is just another way of putting the power of your mind to work for you rather than against you. As I have repeatedly emphasized throughout this book, the mind is a very, very powerful tool when it comes to exacerbating or overcoming your hidden barrier to college success. Visioning, like Cognitive Behavioral Therapy, is yet another way to use your mind in the service of healing. Try it. You may be amazed by how much of what you envisioned actually appears in your life at some point in the future.

REFERENCES

Much of the material contained in this book has been derived from my own studies as a counseling student and/or from my experience as a counselor. However, the following sources, all of which I consulted and cited in various chapters throughout the book, may prove very useful to those of you who wish to do some additional research. Note: All of the research cited in this book was updated in January of 2013, though some of the original sources I accessed in 2010-2011 have not been revised since that time.

Capacchione, L. (2000). *Visioning: Ten steps to achieving the life of your dreams.* New York: J. P. Tarcher/Putnam.

Horowitz, S. & Golembeski, K. (2013). Learning disability basics. Retrieved January 12, 2013, from www.ncld.org.

Mayo Clinic. (2012). Alcoholism. Retrieved January 8, 2013, from www.mayoclinic.com.

Mayo Clinic. (2012). Anorexia nervosa. Retrieved January 10, 2013, from www.mayoclinic.com.

Mayo Clinic. (2012). Anxiety. Retrieved January 10, 2013, from www.mayoclinic.com.

Mayo Clinic. (2012). Bulimia nervosa. Retrieved January 12, 2013, from www.mayoclinic.com.

Mayo Clinic. (2012). Depression. Retrieved January 8, 2013, from www.mayoclinic.com.

Mayo Clinic. (2011). Drug addiction. Retrieved January 5, 2013, from www.mayoclinic.com.

Mayo Clinic. (2011). Complicated grief. Retrieved June 3, 2011, from www.mayoclinic.com.

Mayo Clinic. (2011). Generalized anxiety disorder. Retrieved March 20, 2011, from www.mayoclinic.com.

Mayo Clinic. (2012). Grief: Coping with reminders after a loss. Retrieved January 8, 2013, from www.mayoclinic.com.

Mayo Clinic. (2011). Meditation: A simple, fast way to reduce stress. Retrieved April 21, 2011, from www.mayoclinic.com.

Mayo Clinic. (2011). Positive thinking: Reduce stress by eliminating negative self-talk. Retrieved April 21, 2011, from www.mayoclinic.com.

Mayo Clinic. (2011). Self-esteem check: Too high, too low, or just right? Retrieved January 13, 2013, from www.mayoclinic.com.

Mayo Clinic. (2010). Stress management: Constant stress puts your health at risk. Retrieved August 1, 2011, from www.mayoclinic.com.

Mayo Clinic. (2010). Stress management: Identify your sources of stress. Retrieved August 1, 2011, from www.mayoclinic.com.

Mayo Clinic. (2010). Stress management: Need stress relief? Try the four A's. Retrieved August 1, 2011, from www.mayoclinic.com.

Mayo Clinic. (2011). Stress management: Re-examine your stress reactions. Retrieved August 1, 2011, from www.mayoclinic.com.

Mayo Clinic. (2011). Stress symptoms: Effects on your body, feelings, and behavior. Retrieved August 1, 2011, from www.mayoclinic.com.

Mayo Clinic. (2012). Tai chi: A gentle way to fight stress. Retrieved January 12, 2013, from www.mayoclinic.com.

Mayo Clinic. (2013). Yoga: Fight stress and find serenity. Retrieved January 15, 2013, from www.mayoclinic.com.

National Center for Learning Disabilities. (2013). How ADHD affects learning. Retrieved January 13, 21013 from www.ncld.org.

National Center for Learning Disabilities. (2013). What are learning disabilities? Retrieved January 12, 2013, from www.ncld.org.

National Dissemination Center for Children and Youth With Disabilities. (2011). NICHCY disability fact sheet 7. Retrieved December 20, 2011, from www.nichcy.org.

National Institute of Mental Health. (2012). Anxiety disorders. Retrieved January 11, 2013, from www.nimh.nih.gov.

National Institute of Mental Health. (2011). Depression and college students. Retrieved January 9, 2012, from www.nimh.nih.gov.

National Institute of Mental Health. (2010). Eating disorders. Retrieved January 9, 2013, from www.nimh.nih.gov.

National Institute of Mental Health. (2011). Stress-defeating effects of exercise traced to emotional brain circuit. Retrieved December 4, 2012, from www.nimh.nih.gov.

Orloff, J. (2009). *Emotional freedom.* New York: Harmony Books.

Rabinovitz, R. (2011). Getting access to assistive technology in college. Retrieved January 12, 2013, from www.ncld.org.

Reasoner, R. (2010). The true meaning of self-esteem. Retrieved October 4, 2011, from www.self-esteem-nase.org.

Ruiz, D. (1997). *The four agreements: A practical guide to personal freedom.* San Rafael: Amber-Allen Publishers.

Somers, S. (1999). *365 ways to change your life.* New York: Crown Publishers.

Strauss, C. (2004). *Talking to anxiety.* New York: New American Library.

Wright, J. (2003). *There must be more than this: Finding more life, love, and meaning by overcoming your soft addictions.* New York: Broadway Books.

ABOUT THE AUTHOR

Cheryl Kroll has been a community college professor and counselor for nearly twenty years. She holds advanced degrees in English and counseling and currently resides in Los Angeles, California where she is writing her next book.

CPSIA information can be obtained
at www.ICGtesting.com
Printed in the USA
FSOW02n1207011216
28043FS